The easiest way to learn design patterns

With C# code samples using .NET 6 templates

Fiodar Sazanavets

The easiest way to learn design patterns

With C# code samples using .NET 6 templates

Fiodar Sazanavets

This is a Leanpub book. Leanpub empowers authors and publishers with the Lean Publishing process. Lean Publishing is the act of publishing an in-progress ebook using lightweight tools and many iterations to get reader feedback, pivot until you have the right book and build traction once you do.

© 2022 Fiodar Sazanavets

Tweet This Book!

Please help Fiodar Sazanavets by spreading the word about this book on Twitter!

The suggested hashtag for this book is #designpatterns.

Find out what other people are saying about the book by clicking on this link to search for this hashtag on Twitter:

#designpatterns

Also By Fiodar Sazanavets

SignalR on .NET 6 - the Complete Guide

The easiest way to learn design patterns

I dedicate this book to my dad Dzmitry Sazanavets, who is sadly not with us anymore. Rest in peace.

I also dedicate this book to my wife Olga. Without her support, this book would not have been possible.

Contents

Introduction 1
    What design patterns are 1
    Why would you want to learn design patterns 3
    Why design patterns are hard to learn 4
    The goal of this book 5
    The structure of this book 6

About the author and his mission 9
    Getting in touch 12
    Helping to spread the word 12

Part 1: SOLID principles and why they are important . . 13

1. Single responsibility principle 15
    What is single responsibility principle 15
    The importance of single responsibility principle 16
    The concept of class cohesion 22
    Conclusion 24

2. Open-closed principle 25
    What is open-closed principle 25
    Implementing the open-closed principle in C# 26
    Conclusion 36

3. Liskov substitution principle 39
    Implementing Liskov substitution principle in C# 40

CONTENTS

Conclusion 49

4. Interface segregation principle 51
What is interface segregation principle 51
Importance of interface segregation 52
When NotImplementedException is appropriate 63

5. Dependency inversion principle 65
What is dependency inversion principle 65
Why dependency inversion principle is important 66
Dependency inversion is not only useful in unit tests . . 83

Part 2: The problems that design patterns are intended to solve 85

6. Not knowing what object implementations you'll need ahead of time 87
Suitable design patterns 88

7. Making several exact copies of a complex object 93
Suitable design patterns 94

8. Using many instances of an object while keeping code running smoothly 95
Suitable design patterns 96

9. Using the same single instance of an object throughout the application 101
Suitable design patterns 101

10. Third party components aren't directly compatible with your code 103
Suitable design patterns 104

11. Adding new functionality to existing objects that cannot be modified 105
Suitable design patterns 105

12. Accessing complex back-end logic from the presentation layer 107
    Suitable design patterns 108

13. User interface and business logic are developed separately 111
    Suitable design patterns 111

14. Building a complex object hierarchy 115
    Suitable design patterns 115

15. Implementing complex conditional logic 117
    Suitable design patterns 117

16. Multiple object instances of different types need to be able to communicate with each other 121
    Suitable design patterns 121

17. Multiple stages of processing are needed 125
    Suitable design patterns 125

18. The system is controlled by complex combinations of inputs 129
    Suitable design patterns 129

19. Ability to undo an action that has been applied 131
    Suitable design patterns 131

20. Ability to traverse a collection without knowing its underlying structure 133
    Suitable design patterns 133

21. Creating a family of related algorithms 135
    Suitable design patterns 135

22. Summary of the problems design patterns are intended to solve 139

CONTENTS

Part 3: Design patterns demonstrated in C# 145

23. Design pattern categories 147

Creational design patterns 149

24. Factory Method 151
    Prerequisites 152
    Factory Method implementation example 152
    Benefits of using Factory Method 158
    Caveats of using Factory Method 158

25. Abstract Factory 161
    Prerequisites 162
    Abstract Factory implementation example 163
    Benefits of using Abstract Factory 170
    Caveats of using Abstract Factory 171

26. Builder 173
    Prerequisites 174
    Builder implementation example 174
    Benefits of using Builder 183
    Caveats of using Builder 184

27. Prototype 185
    Prerequisites 186
    Prototype implementation example 187
    Benefits of using Prototype 189
    Caveats of using Prototype 190

28. Singleton 191
    Prerequisites 192
    Singleton implementation example 192
    Benefits of using Singleton 195
    Caveats of using Singleton 195

Structural design patterns 197

29. Adapter ... 199
Prerequisites ... 200
Adapter implementation example ... 201
Benefits of using Adapter ... 206
Caveats of using Adapter ... 207

30. Bridge ... 209
Prerequisites ... 210
Bridge implementation example ... 211
Benefits of using Bridge ... 215
Caveats of using Bridge ... 215

31. Composite ... 217
Prerequisites ... 218
Composite implementation example ... 219
Benefits of using Composite ... 223
Caveats of using Composite ... 223

32. Decorator ... 225
Prerequisites ... 226
Decorator implementation example ... 227
Benefits of using Decorator ... 233
Caveats of using Composite ... 234

33. Facade ... 235
Prerequisites ... 236
Facade implementation example ... 236
Benefits of using Facade ... 243
Caveats of using Facade ... 243

34. Flyweight ... 245
Prerequisites ... 246
Flyweight implementation example ... 246
Benefits of using Flyweight ... 250
Caveats of using Flyweight ... 251

CONTENTS

35. Proxy 253
    Prerequisites. 254
    Proxy implementation example 254
    Benefits of using Proxy 258
    Caveats of using Proxy 259

Behavioral design patterns 261

36. Chain of Responsibility 263
    Prerequisites. 264
    Chain of Responsibility implementation example 265
    Benefits of using Chain of Responsibility 270
    Caveats of using Chain of Responsibility 271

37. Command 273
    Prerequisites. 274
    Command implementation example 274
    Benefits of using Command 279
    Caveats of using Command 280

38. Iterator 281
    Prerequisites. 282
    Iterator implementation example 282
    Benefits of using Iterator 293
    Caveats of using Iterator 293

39. Mediator 295
    Prerequisites. 296
    Mediator implementation example 296
    Benefits of using Mediator 302
    Caveats of using Mediator 302

40. Memento 303
    Prerequisites. 304
    Memento implementation example 304
    Benefits of using Memento 309

Caveats of using Memento 310

41. Observer **311**
    Prerequisites 312
    Observer implementation example 312
    Benefits of using Observer 316
    Caveats of using Observer 317

42. State **319**
    Prerequisites 320
    State implementation example 320
    Benefits of using State 324
    Caveats of using State 324

43. Strategy **325**
    Prerequisites 326
    Strategy implementation example 326
    Benefits of using Strategy 330
    Caveats of using Strategy 331

44. Template Method **333**
    Prerequisites 334
    Template Method implementation example 334
    Benefits of using Template Method 340
    Caveats of using Template Method 340

45. Visitor **343**
    Prerequisites 344
    Visitor implementation example 344
    Benefits of using Visitor 352
    Caveats of using Visitor 352

Epilogue **353**

Introduction

Design patterns are something that you will need to get familiar with as a programmer who works with object oriented languages. And this is primarily because they represent well-defined solutions to common software development problems. So, instead of thinking through all the details of your solution, you can simply check if any of the existing design patterns can be used. You won't have to reinvent the wheel.

As a software developer, you would be familiar with reusable software components, such as methods, functions, public classes, libraries, etc. Well, you can think of design patterns as reusable solutions to common software problems. If you are familiar with which design patterns can solve a specific type of a problem, you will no longer have to come up with a bespoke solution, which could have taken you a significant amount of time to design and implement. All you'll have to do is just pick the mostly suitable design pattern and apply it in a specific way to solve this specific problem. The solution is already there. The time taken to implement it would not be much greater than the time it takes you to type the code in.

If you are new to design patterns, let's go through a quick overview of what they are.

What design patterns are

Design patterns are prescribed ways of implementing solutions to common problems. While every specific implementation of them will be bespoke and only relevant to a specific codebase, they still determine how your code should be structured. A design pattern would tell you how different object types in your code should interact with one another. Specific objects would have specific roles, which are prescribed by a specific design pattern. But a specific implementation of those objects would still be relevant only to a specific problem.

If you will, you can compare the concept of design patterns with Agile principles. For example, if you follow Scrum, you would go through all of the relevant ceremonies (daily standups, sprint reviews, etc.). You would have specific roles (Scrum master, product owner and Scrum team members). You would work in sprints of a specific length. But the problems that you will be solving during your sprints will be very specific to your organization. The actual implementation of Scrum methodology will be bespoke.

Design patterns have been used in object oriented programming for some time. But in 1994, they have been officially classified and described in a book called *Design Patterns: Elements of Reusable Object-Oriented Software*, which was written by Erich Gamma, Richard Helm, Ralph Johnson and John Vlissides, who are collectively known as *The Gang of Four*.

So, in a nutshell, each design pattern prescribes how the objects in your code should be structured and how they should behave. For solutions where multiple objects are involved, it prescribes the role for each object.

Let's have a look at a design pattern called *Strategy* as our example. This pattern is commonly used to make your code easily maintainable and testable in situations where you have complex conditional logic. In this design pattern, you have an class with the role of *Strategy*. This class stores an interface, which has a role of *Context*. There are several classes that implement this interface, each performing a specific behavior. Then, all you do inside your conditional logic is assign a specific *Context* implementation to the *Strategy*. And then, once all conditions have been examined, you just execute some method on the *Context* object which *Strategy* class encapsulates. This will execute the behavior that was specific to a particular condition, as a specific implementation of *Context* was assigned to *Strategy* when a specific condition was hit.

So, the design patterns prescribes roles to objects and how these objects should interact with one another. We have one object with the role of *strategy* and several implementations of an object with the role of *Context*. But what the design pattern doesn't prescribe is what specific behavior should the implementation perform or what data type(s) should it return, if any. It's up to us to decide.

Some design patterns don't even involve multiple objects with different roles. *Singleton* and *Prototype* patterns, for example prescribe how to apply internal logic to an object of and what public members should this object have for other objects to access.

So, why would you use design patterns? Why just not provide a bespoke solution to every problem you face? Well, there are some good reasons why design patterns are better. But the reasons why you would want to learn them go beyond the fact that design patterns merely provide a better solution.

Why would you want to learn design patterns

Design patterns will indeed make you more effective at solving problems. When you have used them for a while, you will intuitively know where to apply them. So, you will not have to spend much time thinking of the solution. You will be able to apply one right away.

Not only will you be able to solve the problem quicker, but your code will be cleaner. It will be more readable, easier to test, and easier to maintain.

Let's go back to our example of *Strategy* pattern. You can, of course, just use a complex conditional logic in a single method of your code. But then imagine how hard it might be to test the logic. Also, if the logic is complex, it might not necessarily be the most readable code.

When *Strategy* pattern is implemented, it solves the problem. But beyond that, it makes your code clean. The original method that contains the conditional logic only selects which *Strategy* to implement. It doesn't do anything beyond that. Easy to read. Easy to test. Each *Strategy* implementation only contains an atomic piece of logic that is responsible for only one action. Easy to read. Easy to test.

But the benefits of knowing design patterns go beyond them being good solutions to common problems. Many reputable organizations ask questions about them during job interviews. The major IT giants almost certainly do. So, not knowing design patterns might prevent you from getting a job in the company of your dreams.

The main problem with design patterns is that they are not necessarily easy to learn. Let's examine why that is.

Why design patterns are hard to learn

Many developers, especially the ones who don't have a lot of software-building experience, struggle with design patterns. But if you do struggle with them, it may prevent you from getting a programming job at a reputable organization. After all, recruiting managers often ask questions about design patterns. Otherwise, not knowing design patterns will make you less effective as a software developer, which will slow down your career progress.

The main reason why design patterns are so hard to learn is because of the way they are normally taught. Usually, if you pick pretty much any book on design patterns or open pretty much any online article about them, it would provide a collection of design patterns that you would need to go through. You would then have to go through each of them, try your best to understand the principles behind it and only then try to figure out how to apply it in a real-life situation.

It's a tedious process that doesn't always bring about the right results. It's not uncommon for software developers to memorize just a handful of design patterns that they have been using in their own projects. The remaining ones have been forgotten as soon as they've been learned. And it's hard to figure out which design pattern applies in which situation if you only remember a handful of them.

The goal of this book

This book provides a different approach. It uses a methodology that makes it easy to learn design patterns. So, you no longer have to brute-force your way through them. The process of effective learning is not about memorization. It's about associations. You learn new things easily when you can clearly see how new facts relate to your existing knowledge. And this is precisely the method that this book is built around.

You won't have to brute-force your way into design patterns. In fact, you won't even start with the design patterns. First, we will go through a list of common problems that software developers are required to solve. Those are the things that every software developer can associate with. Even if you haven't faced a particular type of a problem yet, you will still be able to easily understand its description. For each of these problems, we will go through the design patterns that can solve it. And for each one of them, you will go through its core principle and the description of how it can solve this type of a problem. Only then you will be invited to examine this particular design pattern in detail, so you can understand how to implement it in your own code.

This structure of the book also makes it valuable as a reference book. Even when you don't know or don't remember design patterns, looking them up becomes easy. What you need to find is a description of the type of a problem you are trying to solve. And then you will be able to follow it to find the actual design patterns that you can apply to solve it.

Therefore this book is not only an effective learning tool. It's also a reference book that's incredibly easy to navigate. It's been structured in such a way that you'll be able to find the right answer in seconds.

One important thing to note is that this book doesn't aim to cover absolutely all design patterns that exist out there. It focuses on the classic design patterns that were outlined by *The Gang of Four*. So some of the design patterns that you have heard of might be missing.

However, these classic design patterns formed the foundation for all design patterns that came after. Therefore, if you get familiar with them, you will have no trouble learning any newer patterns.

The structure of this book

This book consists of three parts. It has been structured to facilitate easy learning of design patterns for those who aren't familiar with them.

Part 1: SOLID principles and why they are important

SOLID principles are the most fundamental rules of clean code in object-oriented programming. And all design patterns depend on these principles. This is why, in order to be able to understand design patterns, you need to be familiar with SOLID principles. This is why this is the very first thing that you will learn in this book.

Part 2: The problems that design patterns are intended to solve

This part lists various problem types that software developers commonly face. And for each of these problems, it provides a list of design patterns that can solve it.

This part of the book doesn't provide an in-depth description of each of the patterns. It merely provides a brief overview of what each design pattern does and how it can solve a specific type of a problem.

This part of the book has been structured in such a way to ensure that those developers who aren't yet familiar with design patterns can easily look them up and be able to quickly find the most suitable design pattern for a specific type of problem they are facing.

Part 3: Design patterns demonstrated in C#

The final part of the book breaks down each of the design patterns in depth. It uses C# code samples to demonstrate how you can implement each of the patterns in your own code.

About the author and his mission

My name is Fiodar Sazanavets. I am a senior full-stack software engineer with over a decade of experience. I know how hard it is to become a competent software developer. I've been through this process myself. And I'm passionate about helping other people, so the journey would be easier for them than it was for me.

Design patterns was the subject that I found quite difficult to comprehend when I was a mid-level developer. At that point in time, I had heard about the design patterns. I kind of knew that they would make code cleaner and more maintainable. But there was one problem. I found them to be hard to learn.

No, there wasn't a lack of documentation. On the contrary, there are plenty of books and blog posts that describe what design patterns are and provide code samples of their implementations. But the problem with all of this material is that the way design patterns are usually taught makes them really hard to understand, especially for those developers that have never used them before. If you are a novice and you examine any of the design patterns outside the context that it's used under, it will probably look like the code was over-complicated without any obvious reason. And that's precisely what made it so hard for me to learn the patterns. After all, I have been coding quite happily without using any of them. So I have abandoned my attempts to learn them.

But it all changed one day when I had a technical interview at one of the major IT companies in London. The company was great and the position that I was interviewing for was paying way above the market rate. But I ended up not getting this job. And my lack of knowledge of the design patterns was to blame.

During the technical interview, I was presented with a problem that one of the design patterns could have solved in minutes. In fact, this problem was specifically designed to assess whether or not a candidate knows design patterns. Because I didn't know them, it was taking me a long time to come up with the solution. And I didn't manage to fully implement the solution within the allocated time. So, essentially, I failed for two reasons:

1. I didn't solve the problem quickly enough
2. I didn't know design patterns

Later, I found out that this wasn't just an isolated case. There are plenty of good IT companies that won't hire you if you don't know design patterns. So I got back to trying to learn them.

They were still hard to learn. I had to brute-force my way through them. But I managed to learn them all. Then I started to use them in my job. And this was when I realized how underappreciated they are.

Design patterns aren't needed only to get your foot into the door of a good IT company. A lot of problems that you encounter as a software developer can be solved relatively quickly if you know design patterns. You will also understand open source code better, as plenty of popular repositories use design patterns.

This experience was what inspired me to write this book. My mission is to help as many people as possible with the process of learning design patterns. But I don't want them to brute-force their way through them, like I once did. I want to make the process of learning them as smooth for the reader as possible.

I'm doing it by providing sufficient content first before showing the implementation of each of the design patterns in detail. After all, effective learning is not about trying to memorize things. Effective learning is about building associations between the stuff you already know and the new information you are trying to internalize. Therefore it would be hard to learn design patterns if you just start looking at them without the sufficient knowledge of the context that they are used under.

Without the context, you won't be able to build mental associations. You won't be able to fully understand what each of the design patterns used for. So you will have to fall back to trying to memorize code structures that would probably make little sense to you. And that precisely what makes design patterns seem so hard to learn.

I sincerely hope that you will find this book useful. All the best!

As well as being an author of this book, I have written a number of other technical books and online courses. I regularly write about software development on my personal website, https://scientificprogrammer.net. I am also available to book as a personal programming mentor via https://mentorcruise.com/mentor/fiodarsazanavets.

Getting in touch

If you want to get in touch with me regarding the content of the book, you can contact me via either Twitter or LinkedIn. Perhaps, there is additional content that you want to have included in the next edition of the book. Or maybe you found some errors in the current edition. Any feedback is welcome. And this is how you can get in touch:

Twitter: https://twitter.com/FSazanavets

LinkedIn: https://www.linkedin.com/in/fiodar-sazanavets/

Helping to spread the word

If you found this book useful, please write a review about it on Amazon. This will help the book to be discoverable by more people and will help me, as an author, to produce more quality educational content in the future.

And, of course, if you liked this book, spread the word. Let your friends know about it. This way, you will help more people to become better software developers.

Part 1: SOLID principles and why they are important

Many design patterns were developed with SOLID principles in mind. Therefore it will be hard to learn design patterns unless you know SOLID principles. And this is why the first part of the book will explain what these principles are and will provide some examples of their implementation in C#.

But SOLID principles aren't merely a tool to help you learn design patterns. Every software developer who uses object-oriented programming languages needs to be familiar with SOLID principles and know how to apply them in their daily job. Being familiar with these principles will make you more effective in your job, which will help you to progress in your career. But another thing to remember is that questions about SOLID principles are often asked during technical interviews. So, if you don't know how to apply them, it may prevent you from getting a job that you want.

For those who aren't familiar with what these principles are, SOLID is an abbreviation that stands for the following:

- Single responsibility principle
- Open-closed principle
- Liskov substitution principle
- Interface segregation principle
- Dependency inversion principle

Do you need to always use SOLID principles? Maybe not. After all, principles are not laws. There might be some exceptions where your code would actually be more readable or maintainable if you don't apply them. But to understand whether or not it makes sense not to apply them in any given situation, you first need to understand them. And this is what this part of this book will help you with.

But the important part is that you will struggle to fully understand design patterns unless you understand SOLID principles. SOLID principles are your foundation. Unlike design patterns, they don't apply to any specific type of software development problems. They are fundamental components of clean code. And this is why we will start with them.

1. Single responsibility principle

In this chapter, we will focus on the first of these principles – single responsibility principle. I will explain its importance and provide some examples of its usage in C# code.

Incidentally, as well as being the first principle in the abbreviation, it is also the one that is the easiest to grasp, the easiest to implement and the easiest to explain. Arguably, it is also the most important principle from the list. So, let's go ahead and find out what it is and why you, as a developer, absolutely must know it.

The full solution demonstrated in this chapter is available via the following link:

https://github.com/fiodarsazanavets/Dotnet-CSharp-SOLID-demo/tree/master/1-single-responsibility-principle

What is single responsibility principle

Single responsibility principle states that, for every self-contained unit of code (which is, usually, a class), there should be one and only one reason to change. In more simple language, this means that any given class should be responsible for only one specific functionality.

Basically, your code should be structured like a car engine. Even though the whole engine acts as a single unit, it consists of many components, each playing a specific role. A spark plug exists only to ignite the fuel vapors. A cam belt is there only to synchronize the rotation of the crankshaft and the camshafts and so on.

Each of these components is atomic (unsplittable), self-contained and can be easily replaced. So should be each of your classes.

Clean Code, a book that every developer should read, provides an excellent and easy to digest explanation of what single responsibility principle is and provides some examples of it in Java. What I will do now is explain why single responsibility principle is so important by providing some C# examples.

The importance of single responsibility principle

Those who are familiar with C# will recognize that every C# application has a file that serves as an entry point, which is usually called Program.cs.

Now, let's imagine a basic console application that will read an input text from any specified text file, will wrap every paragraph in HTML p tags and will save the output in a new HTML file in the same folder that the input file came from. If we are to put entire logic into a single class, it would look something similar to this:

```
1   using System.Text;
2   using System.Text.RegularExpressions;
3
4   try
5   {
6       Console.WriteLine("Please specify the file to convert\
7   to HTML.");
8       var fullFilePath = Console.ReadLine() ?? string.Empty;
9       var inputText = ReadAllText(fullFilePath);
10      var paragraphs = Regex.Split(inputText, @"(\r\n?|\n)")
11                          .Where(p => p.Any(char.IsLetter\
12  OrDigit));
```

```csharp
        var sb = new StringBuilder();

        foreach (var paragraph in paragraphs)
        {
            if (paragraph.Length == 0)
                continue;

            sb.AppendLine($"<p>{paragraph}</p>");
        }

        sb.AppendLine("<br/>");
        WriteToFile(fullFilePath, sb.ToString());
    }
    catch (Exception ex)
    {
        Console.WriteLine(ex.Message);
    }
    Console.WriteLine("Press any key to exit.");
    Console.ReadKey();


    string ReadAllText(string fullFilePath)
    {
        return System.Web.HttpUtility.HtmlEncode(File.ReadAll\
    Text(fullFilePath));
    }

    void WriteToFile(string fullFilePath, string text)
    {
        var outputFilePath = Path.GetDirectoryName(fullFilePa\
    th) + Path.DirectorySeparatorChar +
            Path.GetFileNameWithoutExtension(fullFilePath) + \
    ".html";
        using StreamWriter file =
            new(outputFilePath);
```

```
48          file.Write(text);
49      }
```

This code will work, but it will be relatively difficult to modify. Because everything is in one place, the code will take longer to read than it could have been. Of course, this is just a simple example, but what if you had a real-life console application with way more complicated functionality all in one place?

And it is crucially important that you understand the code before you make any changes to it. Otherwise, you will inadvertently introduce bugs. So, you will, pretty much, have to read the entire class, even if only a tiny subset of it is responsible for a particular functionality that you are interested in. Otherwise, how would you know if there is nothing else in the class that will be affected by your changes?

Imagine another scenario. Two developers are working on the same file, but are making changes to completely different pieces of functionality within it. Once they are ready to merge their changes, there is a merge conflict. And it's an absolute nightmare to resolve, because each of the developers is only familiar with his own set of changes and isn't aware how to resolve the conflict with the changes made by another developer.

Single responsibility principle exists precisely to eliminate these kinds of problems. In our example, we can apply the single responsibility principle by splitting our code into separate classes, so as well as having `Program.cs` file, we will also have `FileProcessor` and `TextProcessor` classes.

The content of our `FileProcessor` class will be as follows:

```csharp
namespace TextToHtmlConvertor;

public class FileProcessor
{
    private readonly string fullFilePath;

    public FileProcessor(string fullFilePath)
    {
        this.fullFilePath = fullFilePath;
    }

    public string ReadAllText()
    {
        return System.Web.HttpUtility.HtmlEncode(File.ReadAllText(fullFilePath));
    }

    public void WriteToFile(string text)
    {
        var outputFilePath = Path.GetDirectoryName(fullFilePath) + Path.DirectorySeparatorChar +
            Path.GetFileNameWithoutExtension(fullFilePath) + ".html";

        using var file = new StreamWriter(outputFilePath);
        file.Write(text);
    }
}
```

The content of the `TextProcessor` class will be as follows:

```
1   using System.Text;
2   using System.Text.RegularExpressions;
3
4   namespace TextToHtmlConvertor;
5
6   public class TextProcessor
7   {
8       private readonly FileProcessor fileProcessor;
9
10      public TextProcessor(FileProcessor fileProcessor)
11      {
12          this.fileProcessor = fileProcessor;
13      }
14
15      public void ConvertText()
16      {
17          var inputText = fileProcessor.ReadAllText();
18          var paragraphs = Regex.Split(inputText, @"(\r\n?|\
19  \n)")
20                              .Where(p => p.Any(char.IsLe\
21  tterOrDigit));
22          var sb = new StringBuilder();
23
24          foreach (var paragraph in paragraphs)
25          {
26              if (paragraph.Length == 0)
27                  continue;
28              sb.AppendLine($"<p>{paragraph}</p>");
29          }
30
31          sb.AppendLine("<br/>");
32          fileProcessor.WriteToFile(sb.ToString());
33      }
34  }
```

And this is what remains of our original Program.cs file:

```
1   using TextToHtmlConvertor;
2
3   try
4   {
5       Console.WriteLine("Please specify the file to convert\
6    to HTML.");
7       var fullFilePath = Console.ReadLine();
8       var fileProcessor = new FileProcessor(fullFilePath);
9       var textProcessor = new TextProcessor(fileProcessor);
10      textProcessor.ConvertText();
11  }
12  catch (Exception ex)
13  {
14      Console.WriteLine(ex.Message);
15  }
16
17  Console.WriteLine("Press any key to exit.");
18  Console.ReadKey();
```

Now, the entire text-processing logic is handled by TextProcessor class, while the FileProcessor class is solely responsible for reading from files and writing into them.

This has made your code way more manageable. First of all, if it's a specific functionality you would want to change, you will only need to modify the file that is responsible for that specific functionality and nothing else. You won't even have to know how anything else works inside the app. Secondly, if one developer is changing how the text is converted by the app, while another developer is making changes to how files are processed, their changes will not clash.

While we've split text-processing and file-processing capabilities into their own single responsibility classes, we have left the minimal amount of code inside Program class, the application entry point. It is now solely responsible for launching the application, reading the user's input and calling methods in other classes.

The concept of class cohesion

In our example, it was very clear where the responsibilities should be split. And, in most of the cases, the decision will be based on the same factor we have used – splitting responsibility based on atomic functional areas. In our case, the application was mainly responsible for two things – processing text and managing files; therefore we have two functional areas within it and ended up with a separate class responsible for each of these.

However, there will be situations where a clear-cut functional areas would be difficult to establish. Different functionalities sometimes have very fuzzy boundaries. This is where the concept of class cohesion comes into play to help you decide which classes to split and which ones to leave as they are.

Class cohesion is a measure of how different public components of a given class are inter-related. If all public members are inter-related, then the class has the maximal cohesion, while a class that doesn't have any inter-related public members has no cohesion. And the best way to determine the degree of cohesion within a class is to check whether all private class-level variables are used by all public members.

If every private class-level variable is used by every public member, then the class is known to have maximal cohesion. This is a very clear indicator that the class is atomic and shouldn't be split. The exception would be when the class can be refactored in an obvious way and the process of refactoring eliminates some or all of the cohesion within the class.

If every public member inside the class uses at least one of the private class-level variables, while the variables themselves are inter-dependent and are used in combination inside some of the public methods, the class has less cohesion, but would probably still not be in violation of single responsibility principle.

If, however, there are some private class-level variables that are only used by some of the public members, while other private class-level variables are only ever used by a different subset of public members, the class has low cohesion. This is a good indicator that the class should probably be split into two separate classes.

Finally, if every public member is completely independent from any other public member, the class has zero cohesion. This would probably mean that every public method should go into its own separate class.

Let's have a look at the examples of cohesion above.

In our `TextProcessor` class, we only have one method, `ConvertText`. So, we don't even have to look at the cohesion. It has maximal cohesion already.

In our `FileProcessor` class, we have two methods, `ReadAllText` and `WriteToFile`. Both of these methods use the `fullFilePath` variable, which is initialized in the class constructor. So, the class also has the maximal cohesion and therefore is atomic.

God Object – the opposite of single responsibility

So, you now know what single responsibility principle is and how it benefits you as a developer. What you may be interested to know is that this principle has the opposite, which is known as God Object.

In software development, a method of doing things that is opposite to what best practices prescribe is known as anti-pattern; therefore God Object is a type of an anti-pattern. It is just as important to name bad practices as it is to name good practices. If something has a name, it becomes easy to conceptualize and remember, and it is crucially important for software developers to remember what not to do.

In this case, the name perfectly describes what this object is. As you may have guessed, a God Object is a type of class that is attempting to do everything. Just like God, it is omnipotent, omniscient and omnipresent.

In our example, the first iteration of our code had `Program.cs` file containing the entire application logic, therefore it was a God Object in the context of our application. But this was just a simplistic example. In a real-life scenario, a God Object may span thousands of lines of code.

So, I don't care whether you are religious or not. Everyone is entitled to worship any deity in the privacy of their own home. Just make sure you don't put God into your code. And remember to always use the single responsibility principle.

Conclusion

In this chapter, we have covered the first and arguably the most important SOLID principle of object-oriented software development. In the next chapter, we will have a look at how to use Open-closed principle in the context of C#.

2. Open-closed principle

In this chapter, we will cover the second principle from the SOLID acronym – open-closed principle. We will do so by looking at some examples in C#. However, the general concepts will be applicable to any other object-oriented language.

The full solution demonstrated in this chapter is available via the following link:

https://github.com/fiodarsazanavets/Dotnet-CSharp-SOLID-demo/tree/master/2-open-closed-principle

What is open-closed principle

Open-closed principle states that every atomic unit of code, such as class, module or function, should be open for extension, but closed for modification. The principle was coined in 1988 by Bertrand Meyer.

Essentially, what it means is that, once written, the unit of code should be unchangeable, unless some errors are detected in it. However, it should also be written in such a way that additional functionality can be attached to it in the future if requirements are changed or expanded. This can be achieved by common features of object oriented programming, such as inheritance and abstraction.

Unlike single responsibility principle which almost everyone agrees with, the open-closed principle has its critics. It's almost always obvious how the single responsibility principle can be implemented and what benefits it will provide. However, trying to foresee where the requirements may change in the future and designing your classes in such a way that most of them would be met without having to alter your existing code is often seen as an unnecessary overhead that doesn't provide any benefits.

And the way the software is written has moved on by quite a bit since 1988. If back then the process of deploying a new software version was tedious, long and expensive, many systems of today take minutes to deploy. And the whole process can be done on demand with a click of a mouse.

And with agile software development practices being adopted everywhere in the industry, requirements change all the time. Quite often, the changes are radical. Whole sections of code get removed and replaced on regular bases. So, why design for an adherence to open-close principle if the component that you are writing is quite likely to be ditched very soon?

Although these objections are valid, the open-closed principle still provides its benefits. Here is an example.

Implementing the open-closed principle in C#

In the previous chapter, we had a C# example of single responsibility principle. We have written an application that reads the text from any text file and converts it into HTML by enclosing every paragraph in `p` tags.

After all of the refactoring, we have ended up with three classes, which are as follows. `FileProcessor` class that reads the input file and saves the output into a HTML file:

```csharp
namespace TextToHtmlConvertor;

public class FileProcessor
{
    private readonly string fullFilePath;

    public FileProcessor(string fullFilePath)
    {
        this.fullFilePath = fullFilePath;
    }

    public string ReadAllText()
    {
        return System.Web.HttpUtility.HtmlEncode(File.ReadAllText(fullFilePath));
    }

    public void WriteToFile(string text)
    {
        var outputFilePath = Path.GetDirectoryName(fullFilePath) + Path.DirectorySeparatorChar +
                    Path.GetFileNameWithoutExtension(fullFilePath) + ".html";
        using var file = new StreamWriter(outputFilePath);
        file.Write(text);
    }
}
```

TextProcessor class that processes the text from the input file:

```
1  using System.Text;
2  using System.Text.RegularExpressions;
3
4  namespace TextToHtmlConvertor;
5
6  public class TextProcessor
7  {
8      private readonly FileProcessor fileProcessor;
9
10     public TextProcessor(FileProcessor fileProcessor)
11     {
12         this.fileProcessor = fileProcessor;
13     }
14
15     public void ConvertText()
16     {
17         var inputText = fileProcessor.ReadAllText();
18         var paragraphs = Regex.Split(inputText, @"(\r\n?|\
19 \n)")
20                             .Where(p => p.Any(char.IsLe\
21 tterOrDigit));
22         var sb = new StringBuilder();
23
24         foreach (var paragraph in paragraphs)
25         {
26             if (paragraph.Length == 0)
27                 continue;
28             sb.AppendLine($"<p>{paragraph}</p>");
29         }
30
31         sb.AppendLine("<br/>");
32         fileProcessor.WriteToFile(sb.ToString());
33     }
34 }
```

And Program.cs file that serves as the entry point into the application looks like this:

```
using TextToHtmlConvertor;

try
{
    Console.WriteLine("Please specify the file to convert\
 to HTML.");
    var fullFilePath = Console.ReadLine();
    var fileProcessor = new FileProcessor(fullFilePath);
    var textProcessor = new TextProcessor(fileProcessor);
    textProcessor.ConvertText();
}
catch (Exception ex)
{
    Console.WriteLine(ex.Message);
}

Console.WriteLine("Press any key to exit.");
Console.ReadKey();
```

So far, so good. The application is doing exactly what the requirements say and every element of the application serves its own purpose. But we know that HTML doesn't just consist of paragraphs, right?

So, while we are only being asked to read paragraphs and apply HTML formatting to them, it's not difficult to imagine that we may be asked in the future to expand the functionality to be able to produce much richer HTML output.

In this case, we will have no choice but to rewrite our code. And although the impact of these changes in such a small application would be negligible, what if we had to do it to a much larger application?

We would definitely need to rewrite our unit tests that cover the class, which we may not have enough time to do. So, if we had good code coverage to start with, a tight deadline to deliver new requirements may force us to ditch a few unit tests, and therefore increase the risk of accidentally introducing defects.

What if we had existing services calling into our software that aren't part of the same code repository? What if we don't even know those exist? Now, some of these may break due to receiving unexpected results and we may not find out about it until it all has been deployed into production.

So, to prevent these things from happening, we can refactor our code as follows.

Our `TextProcessor` class will become this:

```
using System.Text;
using System.Text.RegularExpressions;

namespace TextToHtmlConvertor;

public class TextProcessor
{
    public virtual string ConvertText(string inputText)
    {
        var paragraphs = Regex.Split(inputText, @"(\r\n?|\
\n)")
                              .Where(p => p.Any(char.IsLe\
tterOrDigit));
        var sb = new StringBuilder();
        foreach (var paragraph in paragraphs)
        {
            if (paragraph.Length == 0)
                continue;
            sb.AppendLine($"<p>{paragraph}</p>");
        }
        sb.AppendLine("<br/>");
```

```
22          return sb.ToString();
23      }
24 }
```

We have now completely separated file-processing logic from it. The main method of the class, ConvertText, now takes the input text as a parameter and returns the formatted output text. Otherwise, the logic inside of it is the same as it was before. All it does is splits the input text into paragraphs and encloses each one of them in the p tag. And to allow us to expand this functionality if requirements ever change, it was made virtual.

Our Program.cs file now looks like this:

```
1  using TextToHtmlConvertor;
2
3  try
4  {
5      Console.WriteLine("Please specify the file to convert\
6  to HTML.");
7      var fullFilePath = Console.ReadLine();
8      var fileProcessor = new FileProcessor(fullFilePath);
9      var textProcessor = new TextProcessor();
10     var inputText = fileProcessor.ReadAllText();
11     var outputText = textProcessor.ConvertText(inputText);
12     fileProcessor.WriteToFile(outputText);
13 }
14 catch (Exception ex)
15 {
16     Console.WriteLine(ex.Message);
17 }
18
19 Console.WriteLine("Press any key to exit.");
20 Console.ReadKey();
```

We are now calling FileProcessor methods from within this class.

But otherwise, the output will be exactly the same.

Now, one day, we are told that our application needs to be able to recognize Markdown (MD) emphasis markers in the text, which include bold, italic and strikethrough. These will be converted into their equivalent HTML markup.

So, in order to do this, all you have to do is add another class that inherits from TextProcessor. We'll call it MdTextProcessor:

```
namespace TextToHtmlConvertor;

public class MdTextProcessor : TextProcessor
{
    private readonly Dictionary<string, (string, string)>\
 tagsToReplace;

    public MdTextProcessor(Dictionary<string, (string, st\
ring)> tagsToReplace)
    {
        this.tagsToReplace = tagsToReplace;
    }

    public override string ConvertText(string inputText)
    {
        var processedText = base.ConvertText(inputText);

        foreach (var key in tagsToReplace.Keys)
        {
            var replacementTags = tagsToReplace[key];
            if (CountStringOccurrences(processedText, key\
) % 2 == 0)
                processedText = ApplyTagReplacement(proce\
ssedText, key, replacementTags.Item1, replacementTags.Ite\
m2);
        }
```

```
28          return processedText;
29      }
30
31      private int CountStringOccurrences(string text, strin\
32  g pattern)
33      {
34          int count = 0;
35          int currentIndex = 0;
36
37          while ((currentIndex = text.IndexOf(pattern, curr\
38  entIndex)) != -1)
39          {
40              currentIndex += pattern.Length;
41              count++;
42          }
43          return count;
44      }
45
46      private string ApplyTagReplacement(string text, strin\
47  g inputTag, string outputOpeningTag, string outputClosing\
48  Tag)
49      {
50          int count = 0;
51          int currentIndex = 0;
52
53          while ((currentIndex = text.IndexOf(inputTag, cur\
54  rentIndex)) != -1)
55          {
56              count++;
57
58              if (count % 2 != 0)
59              {
60                  var prepend = outputOpeningTag;
61                  text = text.Insert(currentIndex, prepend);
62                  currentIndex += prepend.Length + inputTag\
```

```
63     .Length;
64                 }
65             else
66             {
67                 var append = outputClosingTag;
68                 text = text.Insert(currentIndex, append);
69                 currentIndex += append.Length + inputTag.\
70 Length;
71             }
72         }
73
74         return text.Replace(inputTag, string.Empty);
75     }
76 }
```

In its constructor, the class receives a dictionary of tuples containing two string values. The key in the dictionary is the Markdown emphasis marker, while the value contains the opening HTML tag and closing HTML tag. The code inside the overridden ConvertText method calls the original ConvertText method from its base class and then looks up all instances of each emphasis marker in the text. It then ensures that the number of those is even (otherwise it would be an incorrectly formatted Markdown content) and replaces them with opening and closing HTML tags.

Now, our Program.cs file will look like this:

```
1   using TextToHtmlConvertor;
2
3   try
4   {
5       Console.WriteLine("Please specify the file to convert\
6    to HTML.");
7       var fullFilePath = Console.ReadLine();
8       var fileProcessor = new FileProcessor(fullFilePath);
9
10      var tagsToReplace = new Dictionary<string, (string, s\
11   tring)>
12      {
13          { "**", ("<strong>", "</strong>") },
14          { "*", ("<em>", "</em>") },
15          { "~~", ("<del>", "</del>") }
16      };
17
18      var textProcessor = new MdTextProcessor(tagsToReplace\
19   );
20      var inputText = fileProcessor.ReadAllText();
21      var outputText = textProcessor.ConvertText(inputText);
22      fileProcessor.WriteToFile(outputText);
23  }
24  catch (Exception ex)
25  {
26      Console.WriteLine(ex.Message);
27  }
28
29  Console.WriteLine("Press any key to exit.");
30  Console.ReadKey();
```

The dictionary is something we pass into MdTextProcessor from the outside, so we needed to initialize it here. And now our textProcessor variable is of type MdTextProcessor rather than TextProcessor. The rest of the code has remained unchanged.

So, if we had any existing unit tests on the `ConvertText` method of the `TextProcessor` class, they would not be affected at all. Likewise, if any external application uses `TextProcessor`, it will work just like it did before after our code update. Therefore we have added new capabilities without breaking any of the existing functionality at all.

Also, there is another example of how we can future-proof our code. The requirements of what special text markers our application must recognize may change, so we have turned it into easily changeable data. Now, `MdTextProcessor` doesn't have to be altered.

Also, although we could simply use one opening HTML tag as the value in the dictionary and then just create a closing tag on the go by inserting a slash character into it, we have defined opening and closing tags explicitly. Again, what if the requirements state that we need to add various attributes to the opening HTML tags? What if certain key values will correspond to nested tags? It would be difficult to foresee all possible scenarios beforehand, so the easiest thing we could do is make it explicit to cover any of such scenarios.

Conclusion

Open-closed principle is a useful thing to know, as it will substantially minimize the impact of any changes to your application code. If your software is designed with this principle in mind, then future modifications to any one of your code components will not cause the need to modify any other components and assess the impact on any external applications.

However, unlike the single responsibility principle, which should be followed almost like a law, there are situations where applying the open-closed principle has more cons than pros. For example, when designing a component, you will have to think of any potential changes to the requirements in the future. This, sometimes, is counterproductive, especially when your code is quite likely to be radically restructured at some point.

So, while you still need to spend some time thinking about what new functionality may be added to your new class in the future, use common sense. Considering the most obvious changes is often sufficient.

Also, although adding new public methods to the existing class without modifying the existing methods would, strictly speaking, violate open-closed principle, it will not cause the most common problems that open-closed principle is designed to address. So, in most of the cases, it is completely fine to do so instead of creating even more classes that expand your inheritance hierarchy.

However, in this case, if your code is intended to be used by external software, always make sure that you increment the version of your library. If you don't, then the updated external software that relies on the new methods will get broken if it accidentally received the old version of the library with the same version number. However, any software development team absolutely must have a versioning strategy in place and most of them do, so this problem is expected to be extremely rare.

3. Liskov substitution principle

In this chapter, we will cover Liskov substitution principle. I will explain why this principle is important and will provide an example of its usage in C#.

The full solution demonstrated in this chapter is available via the following link:

https://github.com/fiodarsazanavets/Dotnet-CSharp-SOLID-demo/tree/master/3-liskov-substitution-principle

What is Liskov substitution principle

Liskov substitution principle was initially introduced by Barbara Liskov, an American computer scientist, in 1987. The principle states that if you substitute a sub-class with any of its derived classes, the behavior of the program should not change.

This principle was introduced specifically with inheritance in mind, which is an integral feature of object oriented programming. Inheritance allows you to extend the functionality of classes or modules (depending on what programming language you use). So, if you need a class with some new functionality that is closely related to what you already have in a different class, you can just inherit from the existing class instead of creating a completely new one.

When inheritance is applied, any object oriented programming language will allow you to insert an object that has the derived class as its data type into a variable or parameter that expects an object of the subclass. For example, if you had a base class called Car, you could create another class that inherits from it and is called

SportsCar. In this case, an instance of SportsCar is also Car, just like it would have been in real life. Therefore a variable or parameter that is of a type Car would be able to be set to an instance of SportsCar.

And this is where a potential problem arises. There may be a method or a property inside the original Car class that uses some specific behavior and other places in the code have been written to expect that specific behavior from the instances of Car objects. However, inheritance allows those behaviors to be completely overridden.

If the derived class overrides some of the properties and methods of the subclass and modifies their behavior, then passing an instance of the derived class into the places that expect the subclass may cause unintended consequences. And this is exactly the problem that the Liskov substitution principle was designed to address.

Implementing Liskov substitution principle in C#

In our previous article where we covered the open-closed principle, we have ended up with a solution that reads textual content of a file, encloses every paragraph in P HTML tags and makes conversion of certain Markdown markers into equivalent HTML tags.

And this is what we have ended up with.

We have TextProcessor base class that performs the basic processing of paragraphs in the text that has been passed to it:

```
using System.Text;
using System.Text.RegularExpressions;

namespace TextToHtmlConvertor;

public class TextProcessor
{
    public virtual string ConvertText(string inputText)
    {
        var paragraphs = Regex.Split(inputText, @"(\r\n?|\n)")
                              .Where(p => p.Any(char.IsLetterOrDigit));
        var sb = new StringBuilder();

        foreach (var paragraph in paragraphs)
        {
            if (paragraph.Length == 0)
                continue;
            sb.AppendLine($"<p>{paragraph}</p>");
        }

        sb.AppendLine("<br/>");
        return sb.ToString();
    }
}
```

And we have a class that derives from it, which is called MdTextProcessor. It overrides the ConvertText method by adding some processing steps to it. Basically, it checks the text for specific Markdown markers and replaces them with corresponding HTML tags. Both the markers and the tags are fully configurable via a dictionary.

```
namespace TextToHtmlConvertor;

public class MdTextProcessor : TextProcessor
{
    private readonly Dictionary<string, (string, string)>\
 tagsToReplace;

    public MdTextProcessor(Dictionary<string, (string, st\
ring)> tagsToReplace)
    {
        this.tagsToReplace = tagsToReplace;
    }

    public override string ConvertText(string inputText)
    {
        var processedText = base.ConvertText(inputText);

        foreach (var key in tagsToReplace.Keys)
        {
            var replacementTags = tagsToReplace[key];
            if (CountStringOccurrences(processedText, key\
) % 2 == 0)
                processedText = ApplyTagReplacement(proce\
ssedText, key, replacementTags.Item1, replacementTags.Ite\
m2);
        }
        return processedText;
    }

    private int CountStringOccurrences(string text, strin\
g pattern)
    {
        int count = 0;
        int currentIndex = 0;
        while ((currentIndex = text.IndexOf(pattern, curr\
```

```
36  entIndex)) != -1)
37          {
38              currentIndex += pattern.Length;
39              count++;
40          }
41          return count;
42      }
43
44      private string ApplyTagReplacement(string text, strin\
45  g inputTag, string outputOpeningTag, string outputClosing\
46  Tag)
47      {
48          int count = 0;
49          int currentIndex = 0;
50          while ((currentIndex = text.IndexOf(inputTag, cur\
51  rentIndex)) != -1)
52          {
53              count++;
54              if (count % 2 != 0)
55              {
56                  var prepend = outputOpeningTag;
57                  text = text.Insert(currentIndex, prepend);
58                  currentIndex += prepend.Length + inputTag\
59  .Length;
60              }
61              else
62              {
63                  var append = outputClosingTag;
64                  text = text.Insert(currentIndex, append);
65                  currentIndex += append.Length + inputTag.\
66  Length;
67              }
68          }
69
70          return text.Replace(inputTag, string.Empty);
```

```
71      }
72  }
```

This structure implements the open-closed principle quite well, but it doesn't implement the Liskov substitution principle. And although the overridden ConvertText makes a call to the original method in the base class and calling this method on the derived class will still process the paragraphs, the method implements some additional logic, which may produce completely unexpected results. I will demonstrate this via a unit test.

So, this is a test I have written to validate the basic functionality of the original ConvertText method. We initialize an instance of the TextProcessor object in the constructor, pass some arbitrary input text and then check whether the expected output text has been produced.

```
1   using TextToHtmlConvertor;
2   using Xunit;
3
4   namespace TextToHtmlConvertorTests;
5
6   public class TextProcessorTests
7   {
8       private readonly TextProcessor textProcessor;
9
10      public TextProcessorTests()
11      {
12          textProcessor = new TextProcessor();
13      }
14
15      [Fact]
16      public void CanConvertText()
17      {
18          var originalText = "This is the first paragraph. \
19  It has * and *.\r\n" +
```

```
20                    "This is the second paragraph. It has ** and \
21     **.";
22              var expectedSting = "<p>This is the first paragra\
23     ph. It has * and *.</p>\r\n" +
24              "<p>This is the second paragraph. It has ** and *\
25     *.</p>\r\n" +
26              "<br/>\r\n";
27              Assert.Equal(expectedSting, textProcessor.Convert\
28     Text(originalText));
29         }
30     }
```

Please note that we have deliberately inserted some symbols into the input text that have a special meaning in Markdown document format. However, `TextProcessor` on its own is completely agnostic of Markdown, so those symbols are expected to be ignored. The test will therefore happily pass.

As our `textProcessor` variable is of type `TextProcessor`, it will happily be set to an instance of `MdTextProcessor`. So, without modifying our test method in any way or changing the data type of textProcessor variable, we can assign an instance of `MdTextProcessor` to the variable:

```
1   using TextToHtmlConvertor;
2   using Xunit;
3
4   namespace TextToHtmlConvertorTests;
5
6   public class TextProcessorTests
7   {
8       private readonly TextProcessor textProcessor;
9       public TextProcessorTests()
10      {
11          var tagsToReplace = new Dictionary<string, (strin\
12  g, string)>
```

3. Liskov substitution principle

```
13              {
14                  { "**", ("<strong>", "</strong>") },
15                  { "*", ("<em>", "</em>") },
16                  { "~~", ("<del>", "</del>") }
17              };
18          textProcessor = new MdTextProcessor(tagsToReplace\
19  );
20      }
21
22      [Fact]
23      public void CanConvertText()
24      {
25          var originalText = "This is the first paragraph. \
26  It has * and *.\r\n" +
27              "This is the second paragraph. It has ** and \
28  **.";
29          var expectedSting = "<p>This is the first paragra\
30  ph. It has * and *.</p>\r\n" +
31              "<p>This is the second paragraph. It has ** a\
32  nd **.</p>\r\n" +
33              "<br/>\r\n";
34          Assert.Equal(expectedSting, textProcessor.Convert\
35  Text(originalText));
36      }
37  }
```

The test will now fail. The output from the ConvertText method will change, as those Markdown symbols will be converted to HTML tags. And this is exactly how other places in your code may end up behaving differently from how they were intended to behave.

However, there is a very easy way of addressing this issue. If we go back to our MdTextProcessor class and change the override of ConvertText method into a new method that I called ConvertMdText without changing any of its content, our test will, once again, pass.

```csharp
namespace TextToHtmlConvertor;

public class MdTextProcessor : TextProcessor
{
    private readonly Dictionary<string, (string, string)> tagsToReplace;

    public MdTextProcessor(Dictionary<string, (string, string)> tagsToReplace)
    {
        this.tagsToReplace = tagsToReplace;
    }

    public string ConvertMdText(string inputText)
    {
        var processedText = base.ConvertText(inputText);

        foreach (var key in tagsToReplace.Keys)
        {
            var replacementTags = tagsToReplace[key];
            if (CountStringOccurrences(processedText, key) % 2 == 0)
                processedText = ApplyTagReplacement(processedText, key, replacementTags.Item1, replacementTags.Item2);
        }
        return processedText;
    }

    private int CountStringOccurrences(string text, string pattern)
    {
        int count = 0;
        int currentIndex = 0;
```

```
            while ((currentIndex = text.IndexOf(pattern, curr\
entIndex)) != -1)
            {
                currentIndex += pattern.Length;
                count++;
            }
            return count;
        }

        private string ApplyTagReplacement(string text, strin\
g inputTag, string outputOpeningTag, string outputClosing\
Tag)
        {
            int count = 0;
            int currentIndex = 0;

            while ((currentIndex = text.IndexOf(inputTag, cur\
rentIndex)) != -1)
            {
                count++;
                if (count % 2 != 0)
                {
                    var prepend = outputOpeningTag;
                    text = text.Insert(currentIndex, prepend);
                    currentIndex += prepend.Length + inputTag\
.Length;
                }
                else
                {
                    var append = outputClosingTag;
                    text = text.Insert(currentIndex, append);
                    currentIndex += append.Length + inputTag.\
Length;
                }
            }
```

```
71            return text.Replace(inputTag, string.Empty);
72        }
73 }
```

And we still have our code structured in accordance with the single responsibility principle, as the method is purely responsible for converting text and nothing else. And we still have 100% saturation, as the new method fully relies on the existing functionality from the base class, so our inheritance wasn't pointless.

We are still acting in accordance with the open-closed principle, but we no longer violate the Liskov substitution principle. Every instance of derived class will have the base class functionality inherited, but all of the existing functionality will work exactly like it did in the base class. So, using objects made from derived classes will not break any existing functionality that relies on the base class.

Conclusion

Liskov substitution principle is a pattern of coding that will help to prevent unintended functionality from being introduced into the code when you extend existing classes via inheritance.

However, certain language features may give less experienced developers an impression that it's OK to write code in violation of this principle. For example, virtual keyword in C# may seem like it's even encouraging people to ignore this principle. And sure enough, when an abstract method is overridden, nothing will break, as the original method didn't have any implementation details. But a virtual method would have already had some logic inside of it; therefore overriding it will change the behavior and would probably violate Liskov substitution principle.

The important thing to note, however, is that a principle is not the same as a law. While a law is something that should always be applied, a principle should be applied in the majority of cases. And sometimes there are situations where violating a certain principle makes sense.

Also, overriding virtual methods in C# won't necessarily violate Liskov substitution principle. The principle will only be violated if the output behavior of the overridden method changes. Otherwise, if the override merely changes the class variables that are used in other methods that are only relevant to the derived class, Liskov substitution principle will not be violated.

So, whenever you need to decide whether or not to override a virtual method in C#, use common sense. If you are confident that none of the components that rely on the base class functionality will be broken, then go ahead and override the method, especially if it seems to be the most convenient thing to do. But try to apply the Liskov substitution principle as much as you can.

4. Interface segregation principle

In this chapter, we will have a look at the letter "I" of the SOLID acronym: the interface segregation principle.

The full solution demonstrated in this chapter is available via the following link:

https://github.com/fiodarsazanavets/Dotnet-CSharp-SOLID-demo/tree/master/4-interface-segregation-principle

What is interface segregation principle

In object-oriented programming, interfaces are used to define signatures of methods and properties without specifying the exact logic inside of them. Essentially, they act as a contract that a class must adhere to. If class implements any particular interface, it must contain all components defined by the interface as its public members.

Interface segregation principle states that if any particular interface member is not intended to be implemented by any of the classes that implement the interface, it must not be in the interface. It is closely related to single responsibility principle by making sure that only the absolutely essential functionality is covered by the interface and the class that implements it.

And now, we will see why interface segregation is important.

Importance of interface segregation

We will continue with the same code that we have ended up with after we have implemented the Liskov substitution principle in the previous chapter.

So, we have a base class called TextProcessor that converts paragraphs in the input text into HTML paragraphs by applying relevant tags to them.

```
1   using System.Text;
2   using System.Text.RegularExpressions;
3
4   namespace TextToHtmlConvertor;
5
6   public class TextProcessor
7   {
8       public virtual string ConvertText(string inputText)
9       {
10          var paragraphs = Regex.Split(inputText, @"(\r\n?|\
11  \n)")
12                                      .Where(p => p.Any(char.IsLe\
13  tterOrDigit));
14          var sb = new StringBuilder();
15          foreach (var paragraph in paragraphs)
16          {
17              if (paragraph.Length == 0)
18                  continue;
19              sb.AppendLine($"<p>{paragraph}</p>");
20          }
21          sb.AppendLine("<br/>");
22          return sb.ToString();
23      }
24  }
```

We also have a derived class, MdTextProcessor, that adds a new processing capability – the ability to detect specific Markdown symbols and convert them into corresponding HTML tags. To make sure that any places in the code that accept the original TextProcessor class don't start to behave differently if an instance of MdTextProcessor is passed instead, the additional functionality is implemented via a new method – ConvertMdText.

```
namespace TextToHtmlConvertor;

public class MdTextProcessor : TextProcessor
{
    private readonly Dictionary<string, (string, string)>\
 tagsToReplace;

    public MdTextProcessor(Dictionary<string, (string, st\
ring)> tagsToReplace)
    {
        this.tagsToReplace = tagsToReplace;
    }

    public string ConvertMdText(string inputText)
    {
        var processedText = base.ConvertText(inputText);
        foreach (var key in tagsToReplace.Keys)
        {
            var replacementTags = tagsToReplace[key];
            if (CountStringOccurrences(processedText, key\
) % 2 == 0)
                processedText = ApplyTagReplacement(proce\
ssedText, key, replacementTags.Item1, replacementTags.Ite\
m2);
        }
        return processedText;
    }
```

```
29      private int CountStringOccurrences(string text, strin\
30  g pattern)
31      {
32          int count = 0;
33          int currentIndex = 0;
34          while ((currentIndex = text.IndexOf(pattern, curr\
35  entIndex)) != -1)
36          {
37              currentIndex += pattern.Length;
38              count++;
39          }
40          return count;
41      }
42
43      private string ApplyTagReplacement(string text, strin\
44  g inputTag, string outputOpeningTag, string outputClosing\
45  Tag)
46      {
47          int count = 0;
48          int currentIndex = 0;
49          while ((currentIndex = text.IndexOf(inputTag, cur\
50  rentIndex)) != -1)
51          {
52              count++;
53              if (count % 2 != 0)
54              {
55                  var prepend = outputOpeningTag;
56                  text = text.Insert(currentIndex, prepend);
57                  currentIndex += prepend.Length + inputTag\
58  .Length;
59              }
60              else
61              {
62                  var append = outputClosingTag;
63                  text = text.Insert(currentIndex, append);
```

```
64                     currentIndex += append.Length + inputTag.\
65 Length;
66                 }
67             }
68             return text.Replace(inputTag, string.Empty);
69         }
70 }
```

Currently, neither of the classes implement any interfaces. But we may want to be able to use similar functionality in other classes. Perhaps, we would want to convert input text into different formats, not just HTML. Perhaps, we want to simply be able to mock the functionality in some unit tests. So, it would be beneficial to us to get our classes to implement some interfaces.

As our MdTextProcessor has two methods, ConvertText, which is inherited from TextProcessor and ConvertMdText, which is it's own, we can have an interface like this:

```
1 namespace TextToHtmlConvertor;
2
3 public interface ITextProcessor
4 {
5     string ConvertText(string inputText);
6     string ConvertMdText(string inputText);
7 }
```

And implement it like this:

```
namespace TextToHtmlConvertor;

public class MdTextProcessor : TextProcessor, ITextProces\
sor
{
    private readonly Dictionary<string, (string, string)>\
 tagsToReplace;

    public MdTextProcessor(Dictionary<string, (string, st\
ring)> tagsToReplace)
    {
        this.tagsToReplace = tagsToReplace;
    }

    public string ConvertMdText(string inputText)
    {
        var processedText = base.ConvertText(inputText);

        foreach (var key in tagsToReplace.Keys)
        {
            var replacementTags = tagsToReplace[key];
            if (CountStringOccurrences(processedText, key\
) % 2 == 0)
                processedText = ApplyTagReplacement(proce\
ssedText, key, replacementTags.Item1, replacementTags.Ite\
m2);
        }
        return processedText;
    }

    private int CountStringOccurrences(string text, strin\
g pattern)
    {
        int count = 0;
        int currentIndex = 0;
```

```
            while ((currentIndex = text.IndexOf(pattern, curr\
entIndex)) != -1)
            {
                currentIndex += pattern.Length;
                count++;
            }
        return count;
    }

    private string ApplyTagReplacement(string text, strin\
g inputTag, string outputOpeningTag, string outputClosing\
Tag)
    {
        int count = 0;
        int currentIndex = 0;

        while ((currentIndex = text.IndexOf(inputTag, cur\
rentIndex)) != -1)
        {
            count++;
            if (count % 2 != 0)
            {
                var prepend = outputOpeningTag;
                text = text.Insert(currentIndex, prepend);
                currentIndex += prepend.Length + inputTag\
.Length;
            }
            else
            {
                var append = outputClosingTag;
                text = text.Insert(currentIndex, append);
                currentIndex += append.Length + inputTag.\
Length;
            }
        }
```

```
71
72            return text.Replace(inputTag, string.Empty);
73     }
74 }
```

So far so good. However, there is a problem. If we want to implement this interface in the original `TextProcessor` class, we will now have to add the `ConvertMdText` method to it. However, this method is not relevant to this particular class. So, to let the programmers know that this method is not intended to be used, we get it to throw `NotImplementedException`.

```
1  using System.Text;
2  using System.Text.RegularExpressions;
3
4  namespace TextToHtmlConvertor;
5
6  public class TextProcessor : ITextProcessor
7  {
8      public virtual string ConvertText(string inputText)
9      {
10         var paragraphs = Regex.Split(inputText, @"(\r\n?|\
11 \n)")
12                             .Where(p => p.Any(char.IsLe\
13 tterOrDigit));
14         var sb = new StringBuilder();
15         foreach (var paragraph in paragraphs)
16         {
17             if (paragraph.Length == 0)
18                 continue;
19             sb.AppendLine($"<p>{paragraph}</p>");
20         }
21         sb.AppendLine("<br/>");
22         return sb.ToString();
23     }
```

```
24
25      public string ConvertMdText(string inputText)
26      {
27          throw new NotImplementedException();
28      }
29  }
```

And that introduces a problem. We have ended up with a method that we will never use. And what if we would want to create other derived classes that are designed to deal with text formats other than MD? We will then have to expand our interface and keep adding new unused methods to every class that implements it.

So, we can implement the following solution. Our base interface will only have a single method that the base class will use:

```
1  namespace TextToHtmlConvertor;
2
3  public interface ITextProcessor
4  {
5      string ConvertText(string inputText);
6  }
```

The good news that, in C#, we can use inheritance for interfaces, just like we can use it for classes. So, we can create another interface that will be relevant to those classes that are specific to processing of MD-formatted text:

```
1  namespace TextToHtmlConvertor;
2
3  public interface IMdTextProcessor : ITextProcessor
4  {
5      string ConvertMdText(string inputText);
6  }
```

And so, we would implement the interface by the base class without having to add any new methods:

```csharp
using System.Text;
using System.Text.RegularExpressions;

namespace TextToHtmlConvertor;

public class TextProcessor : ITextProcessor
{
    public virtual string ConvertText(string inputText)
    {
        var paragraphs = Regex.Split(inputText, @"(\r\n?|\n)")
                              .Where(p => p.Any(char.IsLetterOrDigit));
        var sb = new StringBuilder();
        foreach (var paragraph in paragraphs)
        {
            if (paragraph.Length == 0)
                continue;
            sb.AppendLine($"<p>{paragraph}</p>");
        }
        sb.AppendLine("<br/>");
        return sb.ToString();
    }
}
```

And our derived class will remain clean too:

```
namespace TextToHtmlConvertor;

public class MdTextProcessor : TextProcessor, IMdTextProc\
essor
{
    private readonly Dictionary<string, (string, string)>\
 tagsToReplace;

    public MdTextProcessor(Dictionary<string, (string, st\
ring)> tagsToReplace)
    {
        this.tagsToReplace = tagsToReplace;
    }

    public string ConvertMdText(string inputText)
    {
        var processedText = base.ConvertText(inputText);
        foreach (var key in tagsToReplace.Keys)
        {
            var replacementTags = tagsToReplace[key];
            if (CountStringOccurrences(processedText, key\
) % 2 == 0)
                processedText = ApplyTagReplacement(proce\
ssedText, key, replacementTags.Item1, replacementTags.Ite\
m2);
        }
        return processedText;
    }

    private int CountStringOccurrences(string text, strin\
g pattern)
    {
        int count = 0;
        int currentIndex = 0;
        while ((currentIndex = text.IndexOf(pattern, curr\
```

```
36     entIndex)) != -1)
37         {
38             currentIndex += pattern.Length;
39             count++;
40         }
41         return count;
42     }
43
44     private string ApplyTagReplacement(string text, strin\
45   g inputTag, string outputOpeningTag, string outputClosing\
46   Tag)
47     {
48         int count = 0;
49         int currentIndex = 0;
50         while ((currentIndex = text.IndexOf(inputTag, cur\
51   rentIndex)) != -1)
52         {
53             count++;
54             if (count % 2 != 0)
55             {
56                 var prepend = outputOpeningTag;
57                 text = text.Insert(currentIndex, prepend);
58                 currentIndex += prepend.Length + inputTag\
59   .Length;
60             }
61             else
62             {
63                 var append = outputClosingTag;
64                 text = text.Insert(currentIndex, append);
65                 currentIndex += append.Length + inputTag.\
66   Length;
67             }
68
69             return text.Replace(inputTag, string.Empty);
70         }
```

```
71     }
72 }
```

When NotImplementedException is appropriate

In C#, NotImplementedException is an error type that is specifically designed to be thrown from the members that implement the interface, but aren't intended to be used. And it comes directly from the core system library of C#.

At the first glance, it may seem that with this feature in place, the language was designed to violate interface segregation principle. However, there are situations where leaving unused interface methods in your class will be appropriate without necessarily violating this principle.

One situation where throwing NotImplementedException will be appropriate if your class is a work in progress and this has been put there temporarily. You may decide all the essential members for your class ahead of time and create the interface immediately, before you forget what you intended to do.

However, creating the class may take a relatively long time and you may not be able to do it all in one go. Despite this, you will already have to implement every interface member. Otherwise your code would not compile. And gradually, you will populate every member with some valid logic.

This is precisely why Visual Studio populates all auto-generated members with NotImplementedException if you want to auto-implement the interface. Clicking the action button will ensure that your code will compile immediately, while you can populate all the members with whatever logic you want at your own convenience.

And, because every interface member is intended to eventually be implemented and is absolutely required for the finished product, this will not violate interface segregation principle.

The other case is when you want to write an interface implementation to enable easy testing of your code. You may have an original class that is intended to be placed in production. This class may have various pieces of logic that you will not be able to replicate on a development machine. For example, it may be sending requests to a certain server or reading messages from a certain queue. And in that class, every method and property is absolutely required to be there.

However, there may be some pieces of functionality in the class that you would be able to run anywhere. So, you may have a version of the class that only contains those components, which will allow you to easily run certain tests on any machine.

And this is where `NotImplementedException` serves its purpose. In this context, it is there to notify the developer that, although this method or property is an absolutely essential member of the class under normal circumstances, it is not relevant in this specific context.

The alternative would be to mock those methods up. But doing so would give them logic that is completely different from how the production class behaves. Therefore, the behavior you will see in your tests will not be representative of the actual behavior of the deployed software and the tests may be pointless. The methods that are testable, however, will behave exactly as they would in production.

5. Dependency inversion principle

Finally, we've reached the last of the SOLID principles - dependency inversion principle.

The full solution demonstrated in this chapter is available via the following link:

https://github.com/fiodarsazanavets/Dotnet-CSharp-SOLID-demo/tree/master/5-dependency-inversion-principle

What is dependency inversion principle

Dependency inversion principle states that a higher-level object should never depend on a concrete implementation of a lower-level object. Both should depend on abstractions. But what does it actually mean, you may ask?

Any object oriented language will have a way of specifying a contract to which any concrete class or module should adhere. Usually, this is known as an interface.

Interface is something that defines the signature of all the public members that the class must have, but, unlike a class, an interface doesn't have any logic inside of those members. It doesn't even allow you to define a method body to put the logic in.

But as well as being a contract that defines the accessible surface area of a class, an interface can be used as a data type in variables and parameters. When used in such a way, it can accept an instance of absolutely any class that implements the interface.

And this is where dependency inversion comes from. Instead of passing a concrete class into your methods and constructors, you pass the interface that the class in question implements.

The class that accepts an interface as its dependency is a higher level class than the dependency. And passing interface is done because your higher level class doesn't really care what logic will be executed inside of its dependency if any given method is called on the dependency. All it cares about is that a method with a specific name and signature exists inside the dependency.

Why dependency inversion principle is important

We will take our code from where we left it in the previous article about interface segregation principle.

So, we have the `TextProcessor` class that modifies input text by converting it into HTML paragraphs:

```
using System.Text;
using System.Text.RegularExpressions;

namespace TextToHtmlConvertor;

public class TextProcessor : ITextProcessor
{
    public virtual string ConvertText(string inputText)
    {
        var paragraphs = Regex.Split(inputText, @"(\r\n?|\n)")
                        .Where(p => p.Any(char.IsLe\
```

```
13  tterOrDigit));
14          var sb = new StringBuilder();
15
16          foreach (var paragraph in paragraphs)
17          {
18              if (paragraph.Length == 0)
19                  continue;
20              sb.AppendLine($"<p>{paragraph}</p>");
21          }
22
23          sb.AppendLine("<br/>");
24          return sb.ToString();
25      }
26  }
```

It implements the following interface:

```
1  namespace TextToHtmlConvertor;
2
3  public interface ITextProcessor
4  {
5      string ConvertText(string inputText);
6  }
```

We have a more advanced version of TextProcessor that also converts MD tags into corresponding HTML elements. It's called MdTextProcessor and it's derived from the original TextProcessor:

```
namespace TextToHtmlConvertor;

public class MdTextProcessor : TextProcessor, IMdTextProc\
essor
{
    private readonly Dictionary<string, (string, string)>\
 tagsToReplace;

    public MdTextProcessor(Dictionary<string, (string, st\
ring)> tagsToReplace)
    {
        this.tagsToReplace = tagsToReplace;
    }

    public string ConvertMdText(string inputText)
    {
        var processedText = base.ConvertText(inputText);

        foreach (var key in tagsToReplace.Keys)
        {
            var replacementTags = tagsToReplace[key];
            if (CountStringOccurrences(processedText, key\
) % 2 == 0)
                processedText = ApplyTagReplacement(proce\
ssedText, key, replacementTags.Item1, replacementTags.Ite\
m2);
        }

        return processedText;
    }

    private int CountStringOccurrences(string text, strin\
g pattern)
    {
        int count = 0;
```

```
36            int currentIndex = 0;
37
38            while ((currentIndex = text.IndexOf(pattern, curr\
39    entIndex)) != -1)
40            {
41                currentIndex += pattern.Length;
42                count++;
43            }
44
45            return count;
46        }
47
48        private string ApplyTagReplacement(string text, strin\
49    g inputTag, string outputOpeningTag, string outputClosing\
50    Tag)
51        {
52            int count = 0;
53            int currentIndex = 0;
54
55            while ((currentIndex = text.IndexOf(inputTag, cur\
56    rentIndex)) != -1)
57            {
58                count++;
59                if (count % 2 != 0)
60                {
61                    var prepend = outputOpeningTag;
62                    text = text.Insert(currentIndex, prepend);
63                    currentIndex += prepend.Length + inputTag\
64    .Length;
65                }
66                else
67                {
68                    var append = outputClosingTag;
69                    text = text.Insert(currentIndex, append);
70                    currentIndex += append.Length + inputTag.\
```

Length;
            }
        }

        return text.Replace(inputTag, string.Empty);
    }
}
```

It implements the following interface:

```
namespace TextToHtmlConvertor;

public interface IMdTextProcessor : ITextProcessor
{
    string ConvertMdText(string inputText);
}
```

We have `FileProcessor` class that manages files:

```
namespace TextToHtmlConvertor;

public class FileProcessor : IFileProcessor
{
    private readonly string fullFilePath;

    public FileProcessor(string fullFilePath)
    {
        this.fullFilePath = fullFilePath;
    }

    public string ReadAllText()
    {
        return System.Web.HttpUtility.HtmlEncode(File.Rea\
dAllText(fullFilePath));
    }
```
```

```
17
18      public void WriteToFile(string text)
19      {
20          var outputFilePath = Path.GetDirectoryName(fullFi\
21   lePath) + Path.DirectorySeparatorChar +
22                  Path.GetFileNameWithoutExtension(fullFile\
23   Path) + ".html";
24
25          using var file = new StreamWriter(outputFilePath);
26          file.Write(text);
27      }
28  }
```

It implements the following interface:

```
1  namespace TextToHtmlConvertor;
2
3  public interface IFileProcessor
4  {
5      string ReadAllText();
6      void WriteToFile(string text);
7  }
```

And we have Program class that coordinates the entire logic:

```
1   using TextToHtmlConvertor;
2
3   try
4   {
5       Console.WriteLine("Please specify the file to convert\
6    to HTML.");
7       var fullFilePath = Console.ReadLine();
8       var fileProcessor = new FileProcessor(fullFilePath);
9       var tagsToReplace = new Dictionary<string, (string, s\
10   tring)>
```

5. Dependency inversion principle

```
11      {
12          { "**", ("<strong>", "</strong>") },
13          { "*",  ("<em>",     "</em>")     },
14          { "~~", ("<del>",    "</del>")    }
15      };
16
17      var textProcessor = new MdTextProcessor(tagsToReplace\
18  );
19      var inputText = fileProcessor.ReadAllText();
20      var outputText = textProcessor.ConvertMdText(inputTex\
21  t);
22      fileProcessor.WriteToFile(outputText);
23  }
24  catch (Exception ex)
25  {
26      Console.WriteLine(ex.Message);
27  }
28
29  Console.WriteLine("Press any key to exit.");
30  Console.ReadKey();
```

Having all the logic inside the Program.cs file is probably not the best way of doing things. It's meant to be purely an entry point for the application. Since it's a console application, providing input from the console and output to it is also acceptable. However, having it to coordinate text conversion logic between separate classes is probably not something we want to do.

So, we have moved our logic into a separate class that coordinates the text conversion process and we called it TextConversionCoordinator:

```csharp
namespace TextToHtmlConvertor;

public class TextConversionCoordinator
{
    private readonly FileProcessor fileProcessor;
    private readonly MdTextProcessor textProcessor;

    public TextConversionCoordinator(FileProcessor filePr\
ocessor, MdTextProcessor textProcessor)
    {
        this.fileProcessor = fileProcessor;
        this.textProcessor = textProcessor;
    }

    public ConversionStatus ConvertText()
    {
        var status = new ConversionStatus();
        string inputText;

        try
        {
            inputText = fileProcessor.ReadAllText();
            status.TextExtractedFromFile = true;
        }
        catch (Exception ex)
        {
            status.Errors.Add(ex.Message);
            return status;
        }

        string outputText;

        try
        {
            outputText = textProcessor.ConvertMdText(inpu\
```

```
36      tText);
37                      if (outputText != inputText)
38                          status.TextConverted = true;
39                  }
40                  catch (Exception ex)
41                  {
42                      status.Errors.Add(ex.Message);
43                      return status;
44                  }
45
46                  try
47                  {
48                      fileProcessor.WriteToFile(outputText);
49                      status.OutputFileSaved = true;
50                  }
51                  catch (Exception ex)
52                  {
53                      status.Errors.Add(ex.Message);
54                      return status;
55                  }
56
57                  return status;
58              }
59      }
```

It has a single method and returns conversation status object, so we can see which parts of the process have succeeded:

```csharp
namespace TextToHtmlConvertor;

public class ConversionStatus
{
    public bool TextExtractedFromFile { get; set; }
    public bool TextConverted { get; set; }
    public bool OutputFileSaved { get; set; }
    public List<string> Errors { get; set; } = new List<s\
tring>();
}
```

And our Program.cs file becomes this:

```csharp
using TextToHtmlConvertor

try
{
    Console.WriteLine("Please specify the file to convert\
 to HTML.");
    var fullFilePath = Console.ReadLine();
    var fileProcessor = new FileProcessor(fullFilePath);
    var tagsToReplace = new Dictionary<string, (string, s\
tring)>
    {
        { "**", ("<strong>", "</strong>") },
        { "*", ("<em>", "</em>") },
        { "~~", ("<del>", "</del>") }
    };

    var textProcessor = new MdTextProcessor(tagsToReplace\
);
    var coordinator = new TextConversionCoordinator(fileP\
rocessor, textProcessor);
    var status = coordinator.ConvertText();
    Console.WriteLine($"Text extracted from file: {status\
```

5. Dependency inversion principle

```
23     .TextExtractedFromFile}");
24         Console.WriteLine($"Text converted: {status.TextConve\
25  rted}");
26         Console.WriteLine($"Output file saved: {status.Output\
27  FileSaved}");
28
29         if (status.Errors.Count > 0)
30         {
31             Console.WriteLine("The following errors occurred \
32  during the conversion:");
33             Console.WriteLine(string.Empty);
34             foreach (var error in status.Errors)
35                 Console.WriteLine(error);
36         }
37     }
38     catch (Exception ex)
39     {
40         Console.WriteLine(ex.Message);
41     }
42
43     Console.WriteLine("Press any key to exit.");
44     Console.ReadKey();
```

Currently, this will work, but it's almost impossible to write unit tests against it. You won't just be unit-testing the method. If you run it, you will run your entire application logic.

And you depend on a specific file to be actually present in a specific location. Otherwise, you won't be able to emulate the successful scenario reliably. The folder structure on different environments where your tests run will be different. And you don't want to ship some test files with your repository and run some environment-specific setup and tear-down scripts. Remember that those output files need to be managed too?

Luckily, your `TextConversionCoordinator` class doesn't care where the file comes from. All it cares about is that `FileProcessor` returns some text that can be then passed to MdTextProcessor. And it doesn't care how exactly MdTextProcessor does its conversion. All it cares about is that the conversion has happened, so it can set the right values in the status object it's about to return.

Whenever you are unit-testing a method, there are two things you primarily are concerned about:

1. Whether the method produces expected outputs based on known inputs.
2. Whether all the expected methods on the dependencies were called.

And both of these can be easily established if we change the constructor parameters to accept the concrete implementations.

So, we change TextConversionCoordinator class as follows:

```
namespace TextToHtmlConvertor;

public class TextConversionCoordinator
{
    private readonly IFileProcessor fileProcessor;
    private readonly IMdTextProcessor textProcessor;

    public TextConversionCoordinator(IFileProcessor fileP\
rocessor, IMdTextProcessor textProcessor)
    {
        this.fileProcessor = fileProcessor;
        this.textProcessor = textProcessor;
    }

    public ConversionStatus ConvertText()
    {
        var status = new ConversionStatus();
        string inputText;
```

```
19
20             try
21             {
22                 inputText = fileProcessor.ReadAllText();
23                 status.TextExtractedFromFile = true;
24             }
25             catch (Exception ex)
26             {
27                 status.Errors.Add(ex.Message);
28                 return status;
29             }
30
31             string outputText;
32
33             try
34             {
35                 outputText = textProcessor.ConvertMdText(inpu\
36   tText);
37                 if (outputText != inputText)
38                     status.TextConverted = true;
39             }
40             catch (Exception ex)
41             {
42                 status.Errors.Add(ex.Message);
43                 return status;
44             }
45
46             try
47             {
48                 fileProcessor.WriteToFile(outputText);
49                 status.OutputFileSaved = true;
50             }
51             catch (Exception ex)
52             {
53                 status.Errors.Add(ex.Message);
```

```
54          return status;
55        }
56
57        return status;
58    }
59 }
```

If you now compile and run the program, it will work in exactly the same way as it did before. However, now we can write unit tests for it very easily.

The interfaces can be mocked up, so the methods on them return expected values. And this will enable us to test the logic of the method in isolation from any other components:

```
1  using Moq;
2  using TextToHtmlConvertor;
3  using Xunit;
4
5  namespace TextToHtmlConvertorTests;
6
7  public class TextConversionCoordinatorTests
8  {
9      private readonly TextConversionCoordinator coordinato\
10 r;
11     private readonly Mock<IFileProcessor> fileProcessorMo\
12 q;
13     private readonly Mock<IMdTextProcessor> textProcessor\
14 Moq;
15
16     public TextConversionCoordinatorTests()
17     {
18         fileProcessorMoq = new Mock<IFileProcessor>();
19         textProcessorMoq = new Mock<IMdTextProcessor>();
20         coordinator = new TextConversionCoordinator(fileP\
21 rocessorMoq.Object, textProcessorMoq.Object);
```

```
22        }
23
24        // This is a scenario that tests TextConversionCoordi\
25   nator under the normal circumstances.
26        // The dependency methods have been set up for succes\
27   sful conversion.
28        [Fact]
29        public void CanProcessText()
30        {
31            fileProcessorMoq.Setup(p => p.ReadAllText())
32                        .Returns("input");
33            textProcessorMoq.Setup(p => p.ConvertMdText("inpu\
34   t"))
35                        .Returns("altered input");
36
37            var status = coordinator.ConvertText();
38            Assert.True(status.TextExtractedFromFile);
39            Assert.True(status.TextConverted);
40            Assert.True(status.OutputFileSaved);
41            Assert.Empty(status.Errors);
42        }
43
44        // This is a scenario that tests TextConversionCoordi\
45   nator where the text hasn't been changed.
46        // The dependency methods have been set up accordingl\
47   y.
48        [Fact]
49        public void CanDetectUnconvertedText()
50        {
51            fileProcessorMoq.Setup(p => p.ReadAllText())
52                        .Returns("input");
53            textProcessorMoq.Setup(p => p.ConvertMdText("inpu\
54   t"))
55                        .Returns("input");
56
```

```csharp
            var status = coordinator.ConvertText();
            Assert.True(status.TextExtractedFromFile);
            Assert.False(status.TextConverted);
            Assert.True(status.OutputFileSaved);
            Assert.Empty(status.Errors);
        }

        // This is a scenario that tests TextConversionCoordi\
    nator where the text hasn't been read.
        // The dependency methods have been set up accordingl\
    y.
        [Fact]
        public void CanDetectUnsuccessfulRead()
        {
            fileProcessorMoq.Setup(p => p.ReadAllText())
                            .Throws(new Exception("Read error\
     occurred."));

            var status = coordinator.ConvertText();
            Assert.False(status.TextExtractedFromFile);
            Assert.False(status.TextConverted);
            Assert.False(status.OutputFileSaved);
            Assert.Single(status.Errors);
            Assert.Equal("Read error occurred.", status.Error\
    s.First());
        }

        // This is a scenario that tests TextConversionCoordi\
    nator where an attempt to convert the text throws an erro\
    r.
        // The dependency methods have been set up accordingl\
    y.
        [Fact]
        public void CanDetectUnsuccessfulConvert()
        {
```

82   5. Dependency inversion principle

```
 92            fileProcessorMoq.Setup(p => p.ReadAllText())
 93                            .Returns("input");
 94            textProcessorMoq.Setup(p => p.ConvertMdText("inpu\
 95    t"))
 96                            .Throws(new Exception("Convert er\
 97    ror occurred."));
 98
 99            var status = coordinator.ConvertText();
100            Assert.True(status.TextExtractedFromFile);
101            Assert.False(status.TextConverted);
102            Assert.False(status.OutputFileSaved);
103            Assert.Single(status.Errors);
104            Assert.Equal("Convert error occurred.", status.Er\
105    rors.First());
106        }
107
108        // This is a scenario that tests TextConversionCoordi\
109    nator where an attempt to save the file throws an error.
110        // The dependency methods have been set up accordingl\
111    y.
112        [Fact]
113        public void CanDetectUnsuccessfulSave()
114        {
115            fileProcessorMoq.Setup(p => p.ReadAllText())
116                            .Returns("input");
117
118            textProcessorMoq.Setup(p => p.ConvertMdText("inpu\
119    t"))
120                            .Returns("altered input");
121            fileProcessorMoq.Setup(p => p.WriteToFile("altere\
122    d input"))
123                            .Throws(new Exception("Unable to \
124    save file."));
125            var status = coordinator.ConvertText();
126            Assert.True(status.TextExtractedFromFile);
```

```
127          Assert.True(status.TextConverted);
128          Assert.False(status.OutputFileSaved);
129          Assert.Single(status.Errors);
130          Assert.Equal("Unable to save file.", status.Error\
131   s.First());
132        }
133   }
```

What we are doing here is checking whether the outputs are as expected and whether specific methods on specific dependencies are being called. I have used the Moq NuGet package to verify the latter. This is also the library that allowed me to mock interfaces and set up return values from the methods.

And due to dependency inversion, we were able to write unit tests to literally cover every possible scenario of what TextConversionCoordinator can do.

Dependency inversion is not only useful in unit tests

Although I have given unit tests as an example of why dependency inversion principle is important, the importance of this principle goes far beyond unit tests.

In our working program, we could pass an implementation of IFileProcessor that, instead of reading a file on the disk, reads a file from a web location. After all, TextConversionCoordinator doesn't care which file the text was extracted from, only that the text was extracted.

So, dependency inversion will add flexibility to our program. If the external logic changes, TextConversionCoordinator will be able to handle it just the same. No changes will need to be applied to this class.

The opposite of the dependency inversion principle is tight coupling. And when this occurs, the flexibility in your program will disappear. This is why tight coupling must be avoided.

Part 2: The problems that design patterns are intended to solve

This part of the book lists common types of software problems that software developers face. For each of these problems, any suitable design patterns are listed.

In this part of the book, we don't go into each design pattern in detail. There is a brief description of how it's structured, what it does, and why it can solve a specific type of a problem. Then, at the end of this part, we summarize all the problems that we have covered and, for each of them, we summarize the pros and cons of each design pattern that can solve it.

This part of the book serves two purposes. Firstly, it's much easier to learn by association. Software problems are something that every software developer can easily imagine. Some of these problems would be something that they are personally familiar with. Design patterns, on the other hand, are something that won't make a lot of sense right away if you are new to them. This is why we start with the descriptions of the problems first before we learn the actual design patterns.

Secondly, this structure makes it easy to look up suitable design patterns for those who don't know them yet. If you, as a programmer, are facing a challenging problem at work, the last thing that you would want to do is go through the descriptions of all design patterns and try to figure out which ones can help you to solve the problem at hand. What you would want to do is find the description of the problem that you are facing and then use it to look up any suitable design patterns. If there are more than one, you would want to know the pros and cons of each to assess which one of them fits your specific situation better. Only then you would want to know how to actually implement it. And this is what this part of the book facilitates.

So, use this section of the book both as a learning guide and as a reference source.

6. Not knowing what object implementations you'll need ahead of time

Imagine that you have a code that uses a particular object type. The code that uses this object only needs to know the signatures of accessible methods and properties of the object. It doesn't care about the implementation details. Therefore, using an interface that represents the object rather than a concrete implementation of the actual object is desirable.

If you know what concrete implementation your application will be using ahead of time, you can simply apply dependency inversion principle along with some simple dependency injection. In this case, you will know that it's always a particular implementation of the interface that will be used throughout your working code and you will only replace it with mocked objects for unit testing. But what if the concrete implementation of the interface needs to be chosen dynamically based on runtime conditions? Or what if the shape of the object needs to be defined based on input parameters in the actual place where the object is about to be used? In either of these cases, the dependency injection approach wouldn't work.

Let's look at an example of this. Imagine that you are building an application that can play audio. The application should be able to work on both Windows and Linux. And inside of it, you have an interface called IPlayer that has standard methods that an audio player would have, such as Play, Pause and Stop. It is the implementation of this interface that actually interacts with the operating system and plays the audio.

The problem is that Windows and Linux have completely different

6. Not knowing what object implementations you'll need ahead of time

audio architectures; therefore you cannot just have a single concrete implementation of IPlayer interface that would work on both operating systems. And you won't know ahead of time what operating system your application will run on.

Suitable design patterns

Factory Method

Factory Method is a method that returns a type of object that implements a particular interface. This method belongs in a Creator object that manages the lifecycle of the object that is to be returned.

Normally, you would have several variations of the Creator object, each returning a specific implementation of the object that you want. You would instantiate a specific variation of the Creator object based on a specific condition and would then call its Factory Method to obtain the implementation of the actual object.

In our example above, you would have one version of the Creator object that returns a Windows implementation of IPlayer and another version that returns its Linux implementation. The Creator object will also be responsible for initializing all dependencies that your IPlayer implementation needs. Some code block in your application will check which operating system it runs on and will initialize the corresponding version of the Creator object.

Why would you want to use Factory Method

Why bother using Factory Method, if you can just initialize any objects directly? Well, here is why:

- Good use of single responsibility principle. The Creator object is solely responsible for creating only one specific implementation type of the end-object and nothing else.

- The pattern has been prescribed in such a way that it makes it easy to extend the functionality of the output object and not violate open-closed principle.
- Easy to write unit tests, as Creational logic will be separated from the conditional logic.

Abstract Factory

Abstract Factory is a design pattern that uses multiple Factory Methods inside of the Creator object, so you can create a whole family of related objects based on a particular condition instead of just one object.

Let's change the above example slightly. Imagine that our app needs to be able to either play audio or video, so you will need to implement two separate interfaces – `IAudioPlayer` and `IVideoPlayer`. Once again, it must work on either Linux or Windows.

In this case, your Abstract Factory will have a separate method to return an implementation of `IAudioPlayer` and a separate method to return an implementation of `IVideoPlayer`. You will have a version of the Factory that is specific to Windows and another version that is specific to Linux.

It's known as Abstract Factory because it either implements an interface or extends an abstract class. It is then up to the concrete implementation of the Factory to create concrete implementations of the output objects that are both relevant to a specific condition.

Builder

Builder design pattern is similar to Factory Method, but instead of just returning a concrete implementation of an object all at once, it builds the object step-by-step.

6. Not knowing what object implementations you'll need ahead of time

Let's go back to our OS-independent app that plays audio. In the Factory Method example, we had a concrete implementation of the IPlayer interface for each operating system. However, if we would choose to use Builder instead of a Factory Method, we would have a single concrete implementation of the interface that would act as a shell object. Let's call it Player. It will be this type that gets produced in all scenarios, but the concrete parameters and dependencies will be injected into it based on what kind of operating system it's running on.

For example, both Linux and Windows allow you to play audio and manipulate its volume via the command line. On Linux, it will be Bash Terminal. On Windows, it will be either cmd or PowerShell.

The principles are similar. In both cases, you would be typing commands. But the exact commands will be completely different. Plus there are likely to be separate commands for playing audio files and for manipulating audio volumes.

So, in this case, our Player class will simply delegate the playback of audios to operating system components that are accessible via a command line interface. It's only the actual commands that will be different. And this is where a Builder design pattern comes into play.

Builder consists of two main components – Builder and Director. Builder is a class that returns a specific object type. But it also has a number of methods that modify this object type before it gets returned. Director is a class that has a number of methods, each of which accepts a Builder class, calls methods on it with a specific set of parameters and gets the Builder to return the finished object.

So, in our case, imagine that our Builder class for the Player object (which we will call PlayerBuilder) has the following methods: SetPlaybackInterface (that accepts a playback interface instance), SetAudioVolumeInterface (that accepts audio volume interface instance) and BuildPlayer (that doesn't accept any parameters). When we instantiate our PlayerBuilder class, we instantiate a private instance of `Player` class inside of it. Then, by executing `SetPlaybackInterface` and `SetAudioVolumeInterface` methods, we dynamically add the required dependencies to the instance of our `Player` class. And finally, by executing the `BuildPlayer` method, we are returning a complete instance of a `Player` object.

In this case, our Director class will have two methods, both of which accept `PlayerBuilder` as the parameter: `BuildWindowsPlayer` and `BuildLinuxPlayer`. Both of these methods will call all the methods on the `PlayerBuilder` class in the same order and both will return an instance of a `Player` class. But in the first case, the methods will be called with Windows-specific abstractions of the command line interface, it's the Linux-specific abstractions that would be injected into the `Player` instance.

However, unlike either Abstract Factory or Factory Method, Builder is not only used to build an object the implementation details of which can only be made known at runtime. It is also used to gradually build complex objects.

For example, .NET has inbuilt `StringBuilder` class in its core `System` library. This class is used for building a string from several substrings, so you don't have to just keep replacing an immutable string in the same variable.

Why would you want to use Builder

- Good use of single responsibility principle. Each Builder method has its own very specific role and there is a single method on the Director class per each condition.
- Easy to write unit tests. This is facilitated by the single responsibility principle.
- No need to have different versions of a class if only some of its implementation details may change in different circumstances.

Because an object can be built step-by-step, it is the best design

6. Not knowing what object implementations you'll need ahead of time

pattern to decide what the object will be if you have to adjust its properties one by one by multiple steps of a conditional logic.

You can reuse the same code for different representations of the final object.

7. Making several exact copies of a complex object

Imagine that you have an object that you need to copy multiple times. Because it's not a primitive type, you cannot just copy the value of the whole thing into a new variable of the same type. Instead, you would need to instantiate a new object of this type and then copy the value of every field from the original object instance.

That would be fine for simple objects with a relatively small number of fields that contain primitive types, such as integers and Booleans. But what if you are dealing with complex objects with many fields, some of which contain other objects? And what if such an object contains private fields that you also want to be copied, but can't access?

In this case, you would need to write a complex code to make a copy of an object. For private fields in particular, you may also need to run additional logic to instantiate them. This way of doing things adds complexity; therefore it makes the code less readable and vulnerable to errors. Plus, as you will have no direct access to private members of the object, you may not necessarily end up with an exact copy and suffer some undesirable side-effects as the result.

Suitable design patterns

Prototype

Prototype is a design pattern that was created specifically for this problem.

If you have a complex object that is meant to be copied often, you can make it cloneable. And this is exactly what this design pattern enables you to do.

You would have an interface with a method that produces an instance of an object that implements this interface. Usually, such a method will be called `Clone`. And, if you want to make your object cloneable, you just implement this interface when you define the object type.

Inside this method, you will still need to copy the value of every field into the output object. However, this time, you will only have a single place in the entire code base to do it in – the object itself. So, it will be easier to have a close look at it and consider all edge cases. Likewise, you will have full access to the private members of the object, so your copy will be exact.

Why would you want to use Prototype

- All code to copy complex objects is located in one place.
- You can copy private members of the object.
- Any code that needs to generate a copy of the object will only need to call the `Clone` method without having to worry about the details of the cloning process.

8. Using many instances of an object while keeping code running smoothly

Imagine that you have a requirement to use many similar objects in your application. Perhaps, you are building a distributed application based on microservices architecture and each of these objects represents a unique connection to one of your service instances. Or maybe you are interacting with multiple database entries and, for each one of them, you need an object that represents a database connection.

In this situation, purely using inbuilt language features will probably be problematic. You will need to instantiate every single one of these objects. Once the object is out of scope, your runtime will need to get rid of it to free up the memory. Once you need a similar object again, you will instantiate it again. And so on.

If you follow this approach, you will probably experience a performance hit. Instantiating a new object each time you need to use it is a relatively expensive process. The runtime will need to allocate memory for it and populate those chunks of memory with new values.

If you are using similar objects in different parts of the application, you will be required to allocate sufficient memory to each instance of the object. And that may become quite a lot of memory if you need to use many of such instances.

Likewise, when you are instantiating a new object, there is always a cost associated with running the constructor of the object's data type. The more complex constructor logic is, the bigger performance hit you will get.

Finally, when you are no longer using an instance of the object and it gets out of scope, there will be a performance cost associated with garbage collection. Remember that the memory will not be freed straight away. It will still be occupied until the garbage collector has found your object and identified that it is no longer being referenced anywhere.

The latter, of course, doesn't apply to the languages that don't have an in-built garbage collector. However, in this case, you will have to free the memory yourself if you don't want to introduce a memory leak. So, if you are using one of such languages, like C++ or Rust, you will have an additional issue in your code to worry about.

Suitable design patterns

Object Pool

Object pool is a pattern that allows you to reuse the object instances, so you won't have to keep instantiating new objects every time.

You have a single Pool object that stores multiple instances of instantiated objects of a specific type. If any of these objects aren't being used, they are stored inside the Pool. Once something in the code requests an object, it becomes unavailable to any other parts of the code. Once the caller has finished with the object, it gets returned to the Pool, so it can be reused by other callers.

Initially, you will still need to instantiate objects in the Pool. However, when your Pool grows to a reasonable size, you will be instantiating new objects less and less, as there will be a greater chance of finding objects in it that have already been released by their respective callers.

To ensure that the Pool doesn't grow too big, there will be a property that will limit its size. Likewise, a mechanism inside of it will determine which object instances to get rid of and which ones to keep. For example, you don't need an object pool with 1,000 object instances if your application will only ever use 10.

Why would you want to use Object Pool

- Objects are being reused, so you will not get any performance penalty associated with instantiating new objects.
- Object pool maintains its size as needed, so you will not end up with way more object instances than you would ever expect to use.

Flyweight

This design pattern allows multiple objects to share parts of their state. So, for example, if you have a thousand objects, all of which currently have the same values in some of their attributes, this set of attributes will be moved to a separate object and all thousand instances will be referring to the same instance of it.

This allows you to store way more objects in the memory than you would have been able to otherwise. In the case above, instead of having a thousand instances of a particular object type with all their property values in each, you would have thousand basic skeleton objects, each of which occupying only a tiny amount of space in memory. The remaining properties of these objects will be stored in memory only once.

One disadvantage of flyweight, however, is that it makes your code complicated. You will need to decide which parts of the state are shared and which aren't. Also, you will need to do some thinking on the best way of changing the state once it becomes irrelevant to any specific instance of an object.

Based on this, it's recommended to only use flyweight if you absolutely must support systems where the performance of your code would very noticeably decrease otherwise.

Why would you want to use Flyweight

- Squeezing way more information into memory than you would have been able to otherwise.

Prototype

Prototype, which we have already covered in **chapter 7**, can also help to solve this problem. However, unlike Object Pool, it will not give you any performance benefits.

What Prototype will give you in this situation is the ability to create many similar objects without having to go through a complex process of defining their field values each time.

For example, you may have a service that communicates with several instances of the same microservice and each of these instances is presented by an object in the code. Let's say that all microservices are accessed by the same IP address, but a different port. And the rest of the connection parameters are also identical.

In this case, your configuration file may contain all shared connection parameters. And you will only have to go through the configuration once to create the prototype object. After that, to create any new connection objects, all you'll have to do is clone the existing one and change the port number accordingly.

To gain performance benefits, Prototype can be combined with Object Pool. Prototype is especially useful when the objects in the Object Pool are complex.

Why would you use Prototype alongside Object Pool

- The objects in the Pool are much easier to instantiate, as they can now be cloned.

9. Using the same single instance of an object throughout the application

Imagine that you have a requirement to use exactly the same object instance throughout your entire application, regardless of whether the classes that use it can communicate directly with each other or not.

One thing you can do is instantiate it in one place and then pass the instance to every single class. This will work, but it's less than desirable. It means that you will have to write a lot of extra code that will be hard to read and maintain.

Plus, there is nothing that would stop passing a different object reference into a class that uses it, especially if a developer that is currently working on the code doesn't know that the original intention was to keep the reference the same across the board. This will probably introduce some bugs.

Suitable design patterns

Singleton

With this design pattern, the class that you want to have a single instance of will have a static method that will return an instance of this class. Behind the scenes, this method will call a private

9. Using the same single instance of an object throughout the application

constructor the first time you call it, so the class will be instantiated only once. If you call this method again, then the same instance will be returned as was instantiated before.

Otherwise, the class will have no public constructor, so it will not be possible to create a new instance of it by any external code. This will guarantee that, no matter where you are calling the static method from, exactly the same instance of the class will be returned.

Why would you want to use Singleton

- Being able to use the same instance of an object in any part of your application without explicitly passing an instantiated object.
- It will prevent you from creating more than one instance of a particular type.

Object Pool

We have already covered Object Pool in **chapter 8** as a design pattern primarily intended for managing multiple instances of the same object type without incurring much of performance penalty. However, in order to be accessible throughout the application, Object Pool also needs to be a singleton.

So, in the nutshell, to make the most of Object Pool, the class that acts as an Object Pool must also implement the Singleton design pattern.

Why would you use Object Pool as Singleton

- Your entire application shares the same pool of the objects.
- You don't have to instantiate more object instances than strictly needed.

10. Third party components aren't directly compatible with your code

Imagine that you are working with a third party library that returns data in a specific format. The problem is, however, that this is not the data format that the rest of your application works with.

For example, your code may only be working with JSON, while the third party library only delivers data as XML. In this situation, the last thing that you would want to do is rewrite the rest of your code to make it compatible with XML, especially if you don't expect anything other than this library to use XML.

There is also another variety of this problem that you may encounter. Once again, you are dealing with a third party library, but this time, its accessible interface is written differently from how the set of related functionality is written in your application. If this third party library is meant to be able to replace your own components, ideally it should use the same signatures on its accessible members as your own classes are using. Once again, in this case, the last thing you want to do is include special cases into what was meant to be generic code.

It doesn't necessarily have to be a third party library though. It could be your own legacy code that was written a while ago, when either a different philosophy was implemented or modern best practices weren't properly followed. In this case, you cannot just change the legacy components, as it has already been extensively tested and many other components within the system rely on it.

10. Third party components aren't directly compatible with your code

All these examples have one thing in common – you need to work with something that is structurally different from the rest of your code, but making changes to your own code is not desirable.

Suitable design patterns

Adapter

You can think of Adapter as a wrapper class for whatever component you would want to use in your code that is currently incompatible with it. The Adapter class will be accessible by using exactly the same interfaces that are normally used in your code, while internally it will be calling methods on the external component. If it needs to transfer the data, it will do so in a format that is compatible with the rest of your code base.

Basically, Adapter class is analogous to a real-life physical adapter, such as an electric socket plug adapter. As you may know, the US, UK and continental Europe use different electric sockets. So if you are traveling from the US to Europe, you won't be able to just plug your electronic devices in. You will have to get an adapter that has the same input configuration as a wall socket in the US, but has the same output pin configuration as European socket plug.

Why would you use Adapter

- Adapter allows you to isolate interface conversion functionality to only a single place in your code.
- Open-closed principle is enforced
- The access point into the immutable external component is standardized along with the rest of your code.

11. Adding new functionality to existing objects that cannot be modified

Imagine that you have the following situation. There is either some third party library, or your own legacy code that you need to use. And you need to make some changes to its functionality. You would either need to modify the existing behavior, or add some new behavior. But you can't change the components that you are about to use. This is because you either don't have access to the internal code of those components, or simply aren't allowed to make this change.

Or maybe the external component is not fully compatible with your code, so you will need to both make it compatible and then extend it. However, making the component compatible with your code is a different problem that we have already covered. The specific problem that we are looking at now is the ability to extend the behavior of the objects that you can't modify directly.

Suitable design patterns

Decorator

Decorator is a design pattern that is similar to Adapter. Just like with Adapter, the Decorator class acts as a wrapper around the original object. However, instead of changing the interface of the

11. Adding new functionality to existing objects that cannot be modified

original object, it uses the same interface as the existing object. The API will be exactly the same.

You can think of a silencer on a pistol to be analogous to the Decorator design pattern. The original pistol already has a specific configuration that you cannot change. But attaching a silencer to it makes it behave differently. While the silencer is attached, however, the original pistol still remains intact. The silencer can be removed at any point.

So, when you apply the Decorator design pattern, anything in your code that could previously use the original object would still be able to use the Decorator class in its place. And this is precisely because the original structure of the interface was left intact.

Why would you use Decorator

- It will give you the ability to easily add functionality to those objects that you can't modify directly.
- Open-closed principle is enforced.
- You can use it recursively by applying additional decorators on top of the existing ones.
- You can dynamically add responsibilities to an object at runtime.
- Single responsibility principle is applied well, as each decorator can be made responsible for only a single enhanced functionality.

12. Accessing complex back-end logic from the presentation layer

Imagine that you are dealing with a whole range of complex classes, all of which you would need to access from a single layer of your application. It could be, for example, code that has been auto-generated from a WSDL definition. Or it could be some manually written code, where different classes retrieve data from different data sources.

Because you will need to access all of these classes from the same layer within your application, using those classes directly would probably not be the most optimal thing to do. You would need to refer to all of these classes from the other system components that need to access them.

This is especially problematic with auto-generated classes, as you won't be able to easily create abstractions for them. So, you will either have to manually edit auto-generated code (which isn't a good idea), or pass the concrete classes as references into the components that need them (which is also a bad idea and a clear violation of dependency inversion principle).

The problem will become even more apparent if those complex classes are meant to be updated fairly frequently. In this case, you will have to keep updating all the references to them.

Another problem associated with complex logic are operations that are expensive to run. But what if you need to access the results of such operations frequently? Well, luckily, there are design patterns that can help you solve this problem.

Suitable design patterns

Facade

Facade is a class that controls access to a set of complex objects and makes it simple. Most often, just like an Adapter, it would change the access interface into these classes. However, unlike Adapter, it will usually be a wrapper around several of such classes. Or it may be responsible for a diverse set of interactions between a number of moving system parts rather than just converting one type of a call to another type.

Direct interaction with those complex classes is happening only inside the Facade class, so the other system components are completely shielded away from it. All that the client class will be concerned about is calling the specific methods on the Facade. Client doesn't care how Facade delivers what it needs. It only cares that Facade does the job that is expected of it.

And when any of the above-mentioned components needs to be updated, the update in the logic will only need to happen inside the Facade, which will prevent the other parts of the system from having bugs unintentionally introduced into them by forgetting to update the logic.

Why would you use Facade

- A convenient way of simplifying access to a complex subset of the system.
- All other application components are shielded away from having to interact with a complex logic.
- Since all the code that interacts with a complex subsystem is located in one place, it's easier not to miss updates to the logic if any of the subsystem components get updated.

Proxy

Proxy is not suitable for wrapping a complex logic into a simple accessible interface, but it's still suitable for dealing with subsystem components that are not easy to work with directly.

For example, you may be in a situation where you would only need data from a particular service on rare occasions. If this data takes a long time to obtain and it rarely changes, a proxy can be used to access this data once and store it in memory until it changes.

Or you may have a situation where you would need to restrict access to a particular service based either on a specific outcome of business logic or the roles that the user is assigned to. In this case, the proxy would conduct this check before the actual service is accessed.

So, essentially, proxy is nothing other than a wrapper around a class that has exactly the same access interface as the original class, so both classes are interchangeable. Proxy class is there to restrict access to the original class. It can also be used to implement any pre-processing of the request if it's needed before the original class can be accessed. Proxy can implement additional access rules that cannot be added to the original class directly.

Why would you use Proxy

- You can abstract away all complex implementation details of accessing a particular class.
- You can apply additional request validation before you access a particular class.
- You can get it to only access the actual class when it's necessary, which would positively affect the performance.

13. User interface and business logic are developed separately

You have two separate teams working on the application. One team consists of front-end specialists, who are capable of making a really beautiful user interface. The other team isn't as good at building user interfaces, but it's really good at writing business logic.

Also, what you intend to do is make the user interface compatible with several different types of back-end. Perhaps, the user interface is built by using a technology that can run on any operating system, such as Electron, while there are different versions of back-end components available for different operating systems.

Suitable design patterns

Bridge

Bridge is the design pattern that was developed specifically to solve this problem. It is a way of developing two parts of an application independently of each other.

When bridge is used, the UI part of the application is known as interface, while the back-end business logic part of the application is known as implementation. This is not to be confused with interface and implementation as object oriented programming concepts. In this case, both the user interface and the back end would have various interfaces and concrete classes that implement them. So,

13. User interface and business logic are developed separately

what is known as interface doesn't only consist of interfaces and what is known as implementation doesn't exclusively consist of concrete classes.

Usually, bridge is designed up-front and developers agree how the interface and implementation are to communicate with one another. After that, both of these components can be developed independently. One team will focus on business logic, while another team will focus on usability.

With this design, implementations can be swapped. So, as long as the access points of the implementation are what the interface expects them to be, any implementation can be used.

Using different implementations for different operating systems or data storage technologies is one of the examples. However, you can also develop a very simple implementation with faked data for the sole purpose of testing the user interface.

Why would you use Bridge

- You can develop user interface and business logic independently.
- You can easily plug the user interface into a different back-end with the same access points signatures.
- Those who are working on the user interface don't have to know the implementation details of the business logic.
- Open-closed principle is enforced.
- Single responsibility principle is well implemented.

Facade

Facade, which we had a look at in **chapter 12**, can be used in certain circumstances, although it's often less suitable than Bridge.

For example, imagine that you have to access the back-end of the app via WSDL, which would have some auto-generated code associated with it. This is where a Facade class would be helpful, as it will abstract away all complex implementation details of this communication mechanism.

This is applicable to scenarios where the business logic layer is hosted by a third party. But likewise, if, for whatever reason, the business logic and the UI applications cannot be designed together up-front, it also might be a suitable scenario to use Facade. This is especially true when the back-end business logic application has a complex access API.

But if you don't have to deal with the complex contracts between front-end and back-end components, then facade is not the most useful design pattern to solve this specific problem.

Why would you use Facade instead of Bridge

- Easier to implement when the service with the business logic is hosted by a third party.
- Easier to implement when the interface and the implementation cannot be designed up front.

Proxy

Proxy design pattern that we had a look at in **chapter 12** is useful if your application is relatively simple.

Essentially, you may have some back-end classes and their simplified representations that the UI components will interact with. In this case, you may have interchangeable implementations of back-end classes that the same proxies can deal with.

As Proxy delivers results without necessarily relying on the object it is providing an abstraction for, it's especially useful in situations where the back-end service with the business logic is expected to be modified and re-deployed frequently. This way, the UI would still be fully operational even while the back-end is being re-deployed.

Likewise, as the main purpose of Proxy is to deliver results to the client without having to trigger the actual business logic each time, it's a very useful design pattern to implement in a situation where triggering the actual business logic is computationally expensive.

Why would you use Proxy instead of Bridge

- No outage of user-accessible functionality during back-end re-deployment.
- Much better performance when the business logic is computationally expensive.

14. Building a complex object hierarchy

Imagine that you need to construct a structure where objects need to act as containers to similar objects. It could be that you are building a tree-like data structure. Or perhaps you are building a representation of a file storage system where folders can contain files and other folders.

Suitable design patterns

Composite

Composite is a design pattern that allows you to build tree-like structure in an efficient way.

There are two types of classes involved – a leaf class and a composite class. Both of these classes implement the same interface; however a composite class would have more methods on it.

A leaf class is the simplest class in the structure. It cannot have any additional members. A composite class, on the other hand, can have a collection of members, which can be absolutely any type that implements the interface that both leaf and composite classes implement.

Essentially, a composite class can contain other instances of composite class and leaf instances. Therefore, a composite class would have methods that would allow it to manipulate the internal collection of its children, such as Add, Remove, etc.

The best analogy would be a file storage structure. You can think of files as leaf objects and folders as composite objects. A folder can contain other folders and files, while a file is a stand-alone object that cannot contain any other objects.

Why would you use Composite

- Really easy way of building any tree-like structures.
- Different types of members of the tree structure are easily distinguishable.

15. Implementing complex conditional logic

So, you need to implement either a switch statement with several cases or an if-else logic with several conditions.

A traditional way of dealing with this is just to implement specific code under each condition. However, if you are dealing with a complex conditional logic, your code will become harder to read and maintain.

If you have this conditional logic inside a single method, it will probably become quite difficult to write unit tests for this method. And your code will probably violate SOLID principles, as the method will have more than one responsibility. It will be responsible for both making the conditional decisions and executing different types of logic based on those decisions. You may end up having as many responsibilities inside this method as there are conditions in your statement!

Suitable design patterns

Strategy

Strategy is a design pattern where you have a container object, usually referred to as Context, that contains a specific interface inside of it. Strategy is any class that implements this interface.

The exact implementation of a Strategy object inside the Context object is assigned dynamically. So, the Context object allows you to replace the exact implementation of the Strategy object at any time.

Strategy object would usually have one core action method that is defined on the interface and the Context object will have a wrapper method with a similar signature that will call this method on the current Strategy implementation.

So, what you would normally do is write several Strategy implementations, each of which would contain its own version of the method that executes the action. Then, when you need to have any multi-condition logic, all you will do under each condition is pass a particular implementation of the Strategy into the Context class. At the end, you just execute the action method on the Context class.

If you do this, all that your method with the conditional logic will be responsible for is deciding which Strategy to pass into the Context class. And it will be trivial to validate this behavior with unit tests. Then, each Strategy implementation will be solely responsible for its own specific version of the logic that is to be executed, which is also easy to read and write unit tests against.

Why would you use Strategy

- A really easy way of isolating specific conditional behavior into its own method.
- Helps to enforce single responsibility principle by making the code with the conditional statements solely responsible for outlining the conditions.
- It becomes easy to write unit tests against any code with a complex conditional logic.

Factory Method

Factory method, that we already had a look at in chapter **chapter 6**, is also designed to be used in a complex conditional logic, but its usage is different from the usage of Strategy.

Factory Method allows you to generate any object of a particular type and, just like with Strategy, you can decide on the exact implementation of the Factory Method based on conditions. However, there is one subtle, but significant, difference.

Strategy is used for executing a particular behavior or returning a short-lived simple data object, while Factory Method is used for generating a long-lived object that can execute its own logic outside of the Factory Method.

For example, let's imagine that you have two databases – the main database and the archive database. They both store data in exactly the same format, while the data itself is different.

If you would need to decide which database to return the data from at the request time, you would use Strategy. For example, a Boolean value that determines whether or not to get the data from the archive is defined as a part of the request. And then you would select a Strategy implementation depending on whether that value is set to true or false.

If true, you would use the implementation that gets the data from the archive database. If false, you would get the implementation that retrieves the data from the main database. But whichever database the data comes from, it's the same data structure in the code that represents the data.

Now, imagine that you need to decide whether or not to use the archive database at config time. This way, you would have an abstraction that represents a database connection. When you launch the application, a Factory Method will assign the representation of either the main or the archive database to this abstraction depending on the config value. After that, any request will retrieve the data from whichever database was set up by this logic when the application was first launched.

The differences between Factory Method and Strategy

- Strategy is used for conditional execution of a specific action that may involve the retrieval of relatively simple data objects.
- Factory Method is used for conditionally creating long-lived objects that have their own logic.

Abstract factory

Because abstract factory is nothing other than a collection of related Factory Methods, it is applicable in the same way as Factory Method is, but only if you need to obtain a group of related objects rather than a single object.

16. Multiple object instances of different types need to be able to communicate with each other

Imagine that you have a container object that contains other objects of various types. To make it clearer, imagine that the container object is a background of a user interface, while other objects, such as text boxes, buttons, labels, etc. are the components of it.

There are certain events that certain objects need to emit that should be able to affect other objects. For example, clicking a particular button should be able to change a text on specific labels.

The last thing you would want to do in this situation is connect the components directly to each other. If you do that, your code will become excessively complex. It's especially true when you have many elements inside the placeholder and they need to be connected together in arbitrary many-to-many relationships.

Suitable design patterns

Mediator

Mediator is a class that acts as a communication medium between the objects when they don't have a way of communicating with each other directly.

16. Multiple object instances of different types need to be able to communicate with each other

An analogy would be an air traffic control. Airplanes that take off and land at an airport don't communicate directly with each other. But air traffic control sees them all and issues appropriate instructions to each of them based on what other airplanes are doing.

In the example with the user interface, the background layout itself may act as a mediator. Once any of the controls on it emits a specific type of event, the layout class will decide whether this event is something that any other element needs to be aware of and it will notify that element accordingly.

So, none of the elements care about what happens after the event has been emitted. Deciding what to do with the event is a sole responsibility of a single Mediator class. And if any other elements are affected, the Mediator will issue instructions to them accordingly.

Why would you use Mediator

- The sole responsibility of facilitating communication between different objects is taken up by a single class.
- Individual components are much easier to re-use.
- Open-closed principle is easy to enforce.

Observer

Observer design pattern utilizes the concept of publishing and subscribing. Basically, any elements that emit a specific event are publishers and any elements that need to react to the event are subscribers.

So, if you want a specific object to be affected by specific event types or events with specific data values, you can subscribe that object to those events. If you no longer need to get that object to react to those events, you can unsubscribe.

And an object doesn't have to be restricted to being either a publisher or a subscriber. It can be both. Likewise, an object can be a publisher and/or a subscriber for more than one event type.

Why would you use Observer

- You can easily establish relationships between objects at runtime.
- Easy to enforce open-closed principle.
- You can implement it across application boundaries.

17. Multiple stages of processing are needed

Imagine that you need to implement a logic that requires multiple stages of processing, possibly involving conditional logic.

One example of this would be a validation of HTTP request. First, you may want to see whether the incoming request matches any allowed paths in your application. Then, you may want to check whether the user is authenticated. After that, you may want to check whether the user is allowed to access the particular resource that the request was made for. And so on.

In this situation, you may want to short-circuit this flow as soon as you encounter a condition that wouldn't allow the request to proceed any further. For example, if the request was made to a path that doesn't exist, there is no point in checking the user's credentials. Returning 404 page would be sufficient.

Suitable design patterns

Chain of Responsibility

This design pattern was specifically developed to deal with this problem.

Basically, your logic is arranged into a chain of individual components. Each component has a condition that decides whether to move on to the next component or short-circuit the logic then and there.

A good example of this would be an ASP.NET Core middleware pipeline which was designed specifically for the request validation that was described in the example above.

Why would you use Chain of Responsibility

- You can control the order of multi-stage processing.
- You can stop the process at any time if moving on doesn't make sense any longer.
- Each component in the chain is responsible for a specific stage of processing, so the single responsibility principle is easy to enforce.
- Suitable for scenarios where a one-off logical flow needs to be executed.

Builder

Builder design pattern was already mentioned in **chapter 6**. Although it's not designed for the specific request validation example outlined in the problem description, builder is suitable for other types of situations where you need to execute multiple processing stages.

The whole purpose behind Builder is to allow you to build some sort of object step-by-step. So, if you put a Builder implementation via a multi-stage conditional logic, you would end up with a different end product for each unique combination of conditions.

Unlike Chain or Responsibility, however, Builder doesn't have to work with specific steps done in a specific order. For example, if we are to use `StringBuilder` from C# to build a string, we can apply any arbitrary logic to do it. We can perform as many manipulations with it as we want.

Why would you use Builder instead of Chain of Responsibility

- Easier to implement when the order of the processing steps doesn't need to be exact.
- Suitable for scenarios where a reusable object needs to be built.

18. The system is controlled by complex combinations of inputs

Some internal components of your system need to accept requests with instructions to do some actions.

Over time, the structure of the requests is becoming more and more complicated. For example, there may be different objects in your system that end up executing a very similar action, while having a completely different sets of inputs.

This may start causing issues in your code by making it less readable. For example, if different object types end up executing the same action, you may put this action into a base class that all of these objects inherit from. But what if those objects are totally different, so having them inheriting from the same base type wouldn't be appropriate? Also, if you have a large variety of such objects, you may end up with a lot of base classes.

So, your goal is to standardize your requests.

Suitable design patterns

Command

Command is a design pattern where the request is already embedded in the class that executes a particular action. This class is known as a Command and it only contains a single method, which is usually called `Execute`.

130 | 8. The system is controlled by complex combinations of inputs

So, none of the objects will be responsible for generating the request. Once you create a Command, it can be executed from any object. This leaves the Command object with the sole responsibility of executing the action. Otherwise, all the calling objects need to do is call its Execute method.

Usually, Execute method comes with no parameters (perhaps, except for a cancellation token). But you can still populate the Command with some unique values by passing those into its constructor when the Command is created.

Why would you use Command

- Separating the request from the objects making them, which enforces the single responsibility principle.
- Standardizing instructions across your application.
- Ability to implement undo/redo actions.
- Ability to assemble simple instructions into complex ones.
- Easy to schedule instructions.

19. Ability to undo an action that has been applied

Your software needs to be able to include undo functionality, which, these days, is present in most user interfaces that allow you to edit content.

This is a problem that UI developers were required to deal with for decades, and, as such, it can be solved by a number of standardized design patterns.

Suitable design patterns

Memento

Memento is a design pattern that was intended specifically to deal with this problem.

Memento is the name of an object that internally stores a sequence of snapshots. But it doesn't reveal those details to the outside world. The only accessible endpoints that the memento objects would have would be related to the functionality that the originator class, such as an editor, would require. These may include passing a new snapshot into the memento, restoring old snapshots, etc.

Whenever a change is made in a specific object, a new snapshot of this object is created and it's sent to the memento object, which appends it to its internal sequence of other snapshots. Then, if

19. Ability to undo an action that has been applied

needed, the state of the originator can be restored from the history inside the memento.

Why would you use Memento

- Allows to store a full history of changes, so any of the snapshots can be restored easily.
- Object oriented encapsulation is used well.

Command

Command design pattern that we had a look at in **chapter 18** is also suitable for undoing and re-doing actions. To use it in such a way, you would just need to create a history of Command objects and, for each one of them, add the ability to roll it back.

Unlike Memento, Command doesn't manage internal states of the objects. So, it won't be suitable when private fields need to get their values changed while undoing an action. However, commands can be changed in such a way that you save the instructions, but don't save a collection of the actual states. This way, you don't restore previous states. You merely revert previous actions by executing the opposite actions. And this allows you to use the memory more efficiently.

Why would you use Command instead of Memento

- More efficient use of memory, as you don't have to store each individual snapshot.
- The actual steps are easier to trace.

20. Ability to traverse a collection without knowing its underlying structure

You have a fairly complex data structure due to various constraints that you have to overcome. Perhaps, you need to arrange the data into a binary search tree to enable an efficient search algorithm. Or perhaps it's a linked list, as each item in the collection needs to know about the next item.

In any case, the client class that will be using your library would not care about what algorithm you used and how your data is structured. All it cares about is that it can work with the data in your collection.

Suitable design patterns

Iterator

Iterator is a design pattern that hides implementation details of a collection-manipulating algorithm and only exposes some basic methods that enable any external object to work with the collection, such as `MoveNext` and `HasMore`.

So, as far as your client is concerned, the collection you are dealing with consists of sequential flat data, just like an array would be. However, internally, the data structure can be anything but.

20. Ability to traverse a collection without knowing its underlying structure

These days, you will rarely have to implement Iterator yourself, as core system libraries in all major programming languages already have a whole range of collection types that implement iterators. But there are still some scenarios where you need to write a special type of collection yourself. And this is where Iterator would be very useful.

Why would you use Iterator

- Abstracts away complex implementation details of collection management.
- Simplifies the view of the collection to the client.

21. Creating a family of related algorithms

Imagine that you need to create a family of related algorithms. Each of them will have the same parameter types, the same output object type, but would be composed of completely different internal logic.

You can just create many similar methods, but design patterns allow you to achieve your goal in a better way.

Suitable design patterns

Template Method

Template Method is, perhaps, the simplest way of achieving the goal of defining a family of related algorithms.

In a nutshell, Template Method is just a fairly standard usage of a standard object oriented feature of inheritance. You define either a skeleton method without implementation or a method with a default algorithm implementation in your base class. And then, you just inherit from this class and modify the algorithm steps as needed.

There is a caveat though. This design pattern is only suitable for very similar algorithms. Otherwise, if you alter an algorithm behavior significantly, you may be violating Liskov substitution principle.

Why would use Template Method

- The easiest way of creating several related algorithms.

- You can get the clients to only override specific parts of the default algorithm.
- You can store a bulk of your code in the base class.

Visitor

Visitor is a design pattern that allows you to separate algorithms from the objects they operate on. So, you can add new behavior to an object without having to change the object itself.

Visitor is a class that operates on an object but is separate from it. Therefore, because your Visitor is separate from your object, you can define a number of different Visitors if you want to apply different algorithms to your object.

In order for a Visitor to work, a visitor class needs to be able to "visit" the object. And then it can just call and modify the values of any accessible members of the objects. The only components that the Visitor will not have access to are private variables and methods.

Why would you want to use Visitor

- Separating algorithms from the objects they operate on, which enforces the single responsibility principle.
- Can add any new behavior to an object without having to change the object.
- Can have different sets of behaviors that can be applied to objects.
- Visitor class can accumulate a lot of useful information about an object by visiting it.

State

State is a design pattern that makes an object change its behavior when its internal state changes.

For example, think of your mobile phone. If your phone is in a locked state, a particular button would unlock it. However, when the phone is in an unlocked state, the behavior of the same button would be different. Perhaps, it would take you to the homepage.

This design pattern can also include state transition logic, which would be able to undo and redo actions. This is how State can be used in conjunction with Memento.

Why would use State

- Separating object behaviors from the object, which would enforce the single responsibility principle.
- Allows you to implement a state transition logic.
- Allows you to introduce new behaviors to an object easily without violating the open-closed principle.

Strategy

Strategy, as described in **chapter 6** was intended to be used inside a specific set of conditional logic, so, by definition, it is also a way of defining a series of related algorithms.

After all, all strategy objects within the same set will implement exactly the same interface, making this design pattern a suitable solution for this specific problem.

22. Summary of the problems design patterns are intended to solve

This chapter summarizes which design patterns can be used to solve any specific type of a software development problem. It's intended to be a reference guide to help you find the right design pattern quickly.

All problem categories that we have discussed in this section are listed here. For each one of them, all suitable design patterns are provided. If there are multiple design patterns that can solve a problem of a particular type, a one-sentence summary will be provided next to each to help you decide which of them is more suitable to your specific situation.

Not knowing what object implementations you'll need ahead of time

- **Factory Method** - if an object needs to be instantiated in one go
- **Abstract Factory** - if multiple object needs to be instantiated in one go
- **Builder** - if an object needs to be built step-by-step

Making several exact copies of a complex object

- Prototype

Using many instances of an object while keeping code running smoothly

- **Object pool** - facilitates the reuse of pre-instantiated objects
- **Flyweight** - allows you to have a very large number of similar objects without much performance penalty, but makes the code complicated
- **Prototype** - can be combined with Object Pool to make initial creation of the objects easier

Using the same single instance of an object throughout the application

- Singleton

Third party components aren't directly compatible with your code

- Adapter

Adding new functionality to existing objects that cannot be modified

- Decorator

Accessing complex back-end logic from the presentation layer

- **Facade** - simplifies the access interface to the complex logic
- **Proxy** - caches the result of expensive operations

User interface and business logic are developed separately

- **Bridge** - suitable when front-end and back-end can be designed together up-front
- **Facade** - suitable when back-end is hosted by a third party or cannot be designed alongside the user interface up-front
- **Proxy** - prevents services outage during back-end redeployment

Building a complex object hierarchy

- **Composite**

Implementing complex conditional logic

- **Strategy** - facilitates a conditional one-off action
- **Factory Method** - facilitates a conditional creation of a long-lived object
- **Abstract Factory** - facilitates a conditional creation of multiple long-lived objects

Multiple object instances of different types need to be able to communicate with each other

- **Mediator** - easier to implement when communication logic between different objects doesn't expect to be changed
- **Observer** - easier to implement when communication between different objects is expected to change at runtime or during configuration

Multiple stages of processing are needed

- **Chain of Responsibility** - suitable in scenarios where processing steps are pre-defined and a one-off logical flow is executed
- **Builder** - suitable in scenarios where the order of processing stages can be arbitrary and a reusable object is being built

The system is controlled by complex combinations of inputs

- Command

Ability to undo an action that has been applied

- **Memento** - allows you to store the exact snapshots of the state
- **Command** - allows you to revert by performing an opposite action

Ability to traverse a collection without knowing its underlying structure

- Iterator

Creating a family of related algorithms

- **Template Method** - easy to implement, but might violate Liskov substitution principle
- **Visitor** - allows you to separate an object from its behavior and add many differential types of behavior to the objects
- **State** - allows you to change the behavior of an entire object in one go by changing the mode (state) that the object is in
- **Strategy** - suitable when algorithms are selected by conditional logic

Part 3: Design patterns demonstrated in C#

The third and final part of the book will teach you each of the design patterns in detail. You will learn the basic structure of each of the patterns. And then you will be provided with an example of its implementation.

All code samples are provided in C#. We use the .NET 6 template style.

None of the code is copyrighted, so please feel free to use it and modify it as you please.

23. Design pattern categories

The classic design patterns can be split into three distinct categories: **Creational**, **Structural**, and **Behavioral**. And the design patterns in each category do exactly what the name of the category suggests.

Creational design patterns define the ways of creating objects. The following patterns belong in this category:

- Factory Method
- Abstract Factory
- Builder
- Prototype
- Singleton

Structural design patterns prescribe how to structure your objects. These are the patterns that belong in this category:

- Adapter
- Bridge
- Composite
- Decorator
- Facade
- Flyweight
- Proxy

Behavioral design patterns tell us how objects are supposed to behave. This category consists of the following patterns:

- Chain of Responsibility

- Command
- Iterator
- Mediator
- Memento
- Observer
- State
- Strategy
- Template Method
- Visitor

This section of the book is split into sub-sections. Each of these covers a specific category of design patterns.

Creational design patterns

Creational design patterns tell us how objects should be created in particular situations. This section covers the following patterns:

- Factory Method
- Abstract Factory
- Builder
- Prototype
- Singleton

24. Factory Method

Factory Method is used for creating a concrete implementation of a particular abstract type or an interface. This design pattern is applied when a concrete implementation of an object needs to be chosen conditionally.

Factory Method can be summarized as follows:

- There is an interface or an abstract class with multiple concrete implementations. It represent an object that needs to be created (let's call it **Target Object**).
- There is an abstract object (or an interface), known as a **Creator**, or a **Factory** that returns an abstract version of **Target Object**.
- There is a concrete implementation of the **Factory** per each concrete implementation of the **Target Object**.
- When we need to return a specific implementation of the **Target Object**, we initialize a specific implementation of the **Factory** and call the creation method on it.

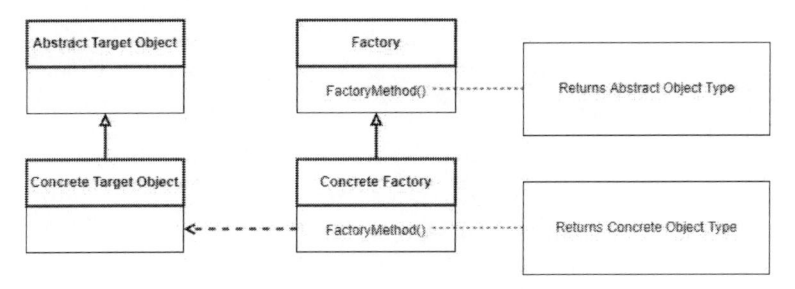

Figure 24.1 - Factory Method UML diagram

We will now go through an example implementation of Factory Method. The complete solution can be found via the link below:

https://github.com/fiodarsazanavets/design-patterns-in-csharp/tree/main/Creational_Patterns/Factory_Method

Prerequisites

In order to be able to implement the code samples below, you need the following installed on your machine:

- .NET 6 SDK (or newer)
- A suitable IDE or a code editor (Visual Studio, Visual Studio Code, JetBrains Rider)

Factory Method implementation example

In our example, we will be building an application capable of playing audio on either Windows or Linux platforms. However, these two operating systems have completely different APIs; therefore they require different code. But our application needs to be able to work on either of them.

To enable this, we need two distinct implementations of audio player functionality. We need a separate implementation for Windows and a separate one for Linux. And this is a scenario that Factory Method is perfect for.

For the demonstration purposes, we will create a console application project. Inside this project, we will add `Player.cs` file with the following content:

```csharp
namespace Factory_Method_Demo;

internal abstract class Player
{
    public abstract Task Play(string fileName);
}
```

This will be the abstract **Target Object**.

Then, we will create an abstract **Factory** object. To do so, we will add PlayerCreator.cs file with the following content:

```csharp
namespace Factory_Method_Demo;

internal abstract class PlayerCreator
{
    public abstract Player CreatePlayer();
}
```

As you can see, we have the CreatePlayer method, which will return an implementation of Player, the abstract class we've created earlier.

Let's now add some concrete implementations. We will first add Linux-specific implementation of the Player class. To do so, we will create LinuxPlayer.cs file and populate it with the following content:

```csharp
using System.Diagnostics;

namespace Factory_Method_Demo;

internal class LinuxPlayer : Player
{
    public override Task Play(string fileName)
    {
        StartBashProcess($"mpg123 -q '{fileName}'");
        return Task.CompletedTask;
    }

    private void StartBashProcess(string command)
    {
        var escapedArgs = command.Replace("\"", "\\\"");

        var process = new Process()
        {
            StartInfo = new ProcessStartInfo
            {
                FileName = "/bin/bash",
                Arguments = $"-c \"{escapedArgs}\"",
                RedirectStandardOutput = true,
                RedirectStandardInput = true,
                UseShellExecute = false,
                CreateNoWindow = true,
            }
        };

        process.Start();
    }
}
```

Then, we will add a Windows-specific implementation of Player. We will call the file WindowsPlayer.cs and add the following content to it:

```
1   using System.Runtime.InteropServices;
2   using System.Text;
3
4   namespace Factory_Method_Demo;
5
6   internal class WindowsPlayer : Player
7   {
8       [DllImport("winmm.dll")]
9       private static extern int mciSendString(string comman\
10  d, StringBuilder stringReturn, int returnLength, IntPtr h\
11  wndCallback);
12
13      public override Task Play(string fileName)
14      {
15          var sb = new StringBuilder();
16          var result = mciSendString($"Play {fileName}", sb\
17  , 1024 * 1024, IntPtr.Zero);
18          Console.WriteLine(result);
19          return Task.CompletedTask;
20      }
21  }
```

As you can see, these two audio player implementations are completely different. But because they both implement the same abstract class, we will be able to apply any implementation that we need. To do so, we will need to create a concrete **Factory** implementation per each of these types. We will first add LinuxPlayerCreator.cs file with the following content:

```csharp
namespace Factory_Method_Demo;

internal class LinuxPlayerCreator : PlayerCreator
{
    public override Player CreatePlayer()
    {
        return new LinuxPlayer();
    }
}
```

Then, we will add WindowsPlayerCreator.cs file with the following content:

```csharp
namespace Factory_Method_Demo;

internal class WindowsPlayerCreator : PlayerCreator
{
    public override Player CreatePlayer()
    {
        return new WindowsPlayer();
    }
}
```

Now, all we need to do is implement our audio playback logic. And to do so, we will replace the content of Program.cs file with the following:

```csharp
using Factory_Method_Demo;
using System.Runtime.InteropServices;

PlayerCreator? playerFactory;

if (RuntimeInformation.IsOSPlatform(OSPlatform.Windows))
    playerFactory = new WindowsPlayerCreator();
else if (RuntimeInformation.IsOSPlatform(OSPlatform.Linux\
))
    playerFactory = new LinuxPlayerCreator();
else
    throw new Exception("Only Linux and Windows operating\
 systems are supported.");

Console.WriteLine("Please specify the path to the file to\
 play");

var filePath = Console.ReadLine() ?? string.Empty;
playerFactory.CreatePlayer().Play(filePath);

Console.ReadKey();
```

So, as you can see, we are using inbuilt operating system detector to conditionally choose the concrete implementation of the **Factory**. Then, we type a path to the file that we want to play and the software will play it. User doesn't need to care what operating system the software is on. It will work exactly the same.

And this concludes our example of Factory Method implementation. Let's now have a look at the specific benefits we gain from using this design pattern.

Benefits of using Factory Method

Why do we need to bother with different implementations of **Target Object**? Why can't we just conditionally apply the functionality that this object encapsulates? Well, here are the reasons why:

- Factory Method enforces the single responsibility principle by separating conditional logic from implementation of the logic inside each condition.
- This allows us to easily maintain the code and write automated tests for it. There won't be any complex and barely readable tests assessing complex conditional logic. Instead, a couple of simple scenarios will asses that the correct implementations of **Target Object** and **Factory** is picked up for each condition. Then, separate sets of scenarios can be applied to each separate **Target Object** and **Factory** implementation.
- Factory Method allows you to execute a particular condition once. Because all implementations of **Target Object** use a common abstraction, a concrete implementation of it can be created once and then just re-used throughout the code.

But this design pattern comes with some obvious caveats too. And this is what we'll have a look at next.

Caveats of using Factory Method

Even with all its benefits in place, you may still question this design pattern. Why do we even need a **Factory**? Why can't we just conditionally select a concrete implementation of **Target Object** directly? Won't it achieve the same benefits with less complexity?

Well, if you have this question, you are right to an extent. If you have a single Factory Method in your **Creator** that returns only one type of a concrete implementation of the **Target Object**, you will gain no benefits of using a **Creator**. But the benefits of Factory Method become really apparent if you have more than one Factory Method in your **Creator** and you are able to return multiple related objects.

Using Factory Method this way turns it into another design pattern, known as Abstract Factory. And this is what we will have a look at next.

25. Abstract Factory

Abstract Factory is closely related to Factory Method. In fact, it is the Factory class that hosts the so-called Factory Method. But as Factory Method refers to a specific method inside a Creator or a Factory class, Abstract Factory can have a number of such methods.

Abstract Factory, along with its Factory Methods, is used for creating concrete implementations of abstract types or interfaces. This design pattern is applied when a concrete implementation of an object needs to be chosen conditionally. But because Abstract Factory can host multiple Factory Methods, it can be used to create concrete implementations of multiple related objects.

Abstract Factory can be summarized as follows:

- There are some interfaces or abstract classes, each having multiple concrete implementations. They represent the objects that needs to be created (let's call them **Target Objects**).
- There is an abstract object (or an interface), known as a **Creator**, or a **Factory** that returns abstract versions of **Target Objects**. Each of these **Target Object** types has a creation method inside the **Factory** associated with it.
- There are multiple concrete implementations of the **Factory**, each returning a specific set of the **Target Object** implementations.
- When we need to return a specific set of the **Target Object** implementations, we initialize a specific implementation of the **Factory** and call the creation methods on it.

25. Abstract Factory

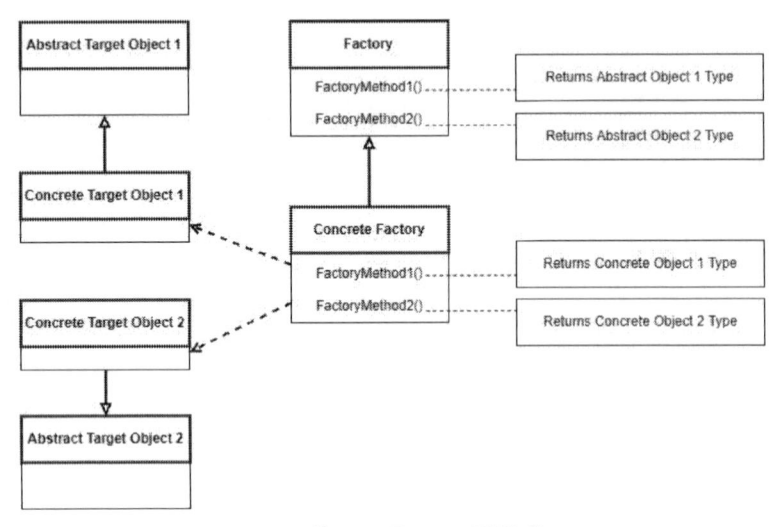

Figure 25.1 - Abstract Factory UML diagram

We will now go through an example implementation of Abstract Factory. The complete solution can be found via the link below:

https://github.com/fiodarsazanavets/design-patterns-in-csharp/tree/main/Creational_Patterns/Abstract-Factory

Prerequisites

In order to be able to implement the code samples below, you need the following installed on your machine:

- .NET 6 SDK (or newer)
- A suitable IDE or a code editor (Visual Studio, Visual Studio Code, JetBrains Rider)

Abstract Factory implementation example

In this example, we will be creating an audio player application that will be able to play audios on either Windows or Linux. It is similar to what we have done when we had a look at an implementation of Factory Method. However, there will be some crucial differences.

In the example that we have used to demonstrate Factory Method, we have been returning a concrete OS-specific implementation of an audio player depending on which operating system the software runs on. This time, however, we will be returning concrete implementations of OS-specific individual functionalities. We will have an object that will provide an abstraction for the Play button and another object that will provide an abstraction for the Stop button.

We will start by creating a .NET console application project. Then, we will add `LinuxPlayerUtility.cs` file to the project and populate it with the following content:

```
using System.Diagnostics;

namespace Abstract_Factory_Demo
{
    internal static class LinuxPlayerUtility
    {
        public static Process? PlaybackProcess { get; set\
; }

        public static void StartBashProcess(string comman\
d)
        {
            var escapedArgs = command.Replace("\"", "\\\"\
");
```

```
15
16                 var process = new Process()
17                 {
18                     StartInfo = new ProcessStartInfo
19                     {
20                         FileName = "/bin/bash",
21                         Arguments = $"-c \"{escapedArgs}\"",
22                         RedirectStandardOutput = true,
23                         RedirectStandardInput = true,
24                         UseShellExecute = false,
25                         CreateNoWindow = true,
26                     }
27                 };
28
29                 process.Start();
30             }
31         }
32 }
```

This will be a static utility class with some functionality shared by Linux-specific implementations of **Target Objects**. We will then do the same for Windows-specific implementations. To do so, we will create `WindowsPlayerUtility.cs` file and populate it with the following content:

```
1  using System.Runtime.InteropServices;
2  using System.Text;
3
4  namespace Abstract_Factory_Demo;
5
6  internal static class WindowsPlayerUtility
7  {
8      [DllImport("winmm.dll")]
9      private static extern int mciSendString(string comman\
10 d,
```

```
11          StringBuilder stringReturn,
12          int returnLength,
13          IntPtr hwndCallback);
14
15      public static void ExecuteMciCommand(string commandSt\
16   ring)
17      {
18          var sb = new StringBuilder();
19          var result = mciSendString(commandString, sb, 102\
20   4 * 1024, IntPtr.Zero);
21          Console.WriteLine(result);
22      }
23   }
```

Now, we will add an abstraction of the Play button. We will create PlayButton.cs file and add the following content to it:

```
1   namespace Abstract_Factory_Demo;
2
3   internal abstract class PlayButton
4   {
5       public abstract Task Play(string fileName);
6   }
```

We will do the same for an abstraction of the Stop button. The file will be called StopButton.cs and its content will be as follows:

```
1   namespace Abstract_Factory_Demo;
2
3   internal abstract class StopButton
4   {
5       public abstract Task Stop(string fileName);
6   }
```

We will then start adding concrete OS-specific implementations of these abstract classes. For PlayButton, we will add LinuxPlayButton.cs file with the following content:

```
namespace Abstract_Factory_Demo;

internal class LinuxPlayButton : PlayButton
{
    public override Task Play(string fileName)
    {
        LinuxPlayerUtility.StartBashProcess($"mpg123 -q '\
{fileName}'");
        return Task.CompletedTask;
    }
}
```

And we will add WindowsPlayButton.cs file with the following content:

```
namespace Abstract_Factory_Demo;

internal class WindowsPlayButton : PlayButton
{
    public override Task Play(string fileName)
    {
        WindowsPlayerUtility.ExecuteMciCommand($"Play {fi\
leName}");
        return Task.CompletedTask;
    }
}
```

We will then add concrete implementations for StopButton. Our LinuxStopButton.cs file will contain the following code:

```
1  namespace Abstract_Factory_Demo;
2
3  internal class LinuxStopButton : StopButton
4  {
5      public override Task Stop(string fileName)
6      {
7          if (LinuxPlayerUtility.PlaybackProcess != null)
8          {
9              LinuxPlayerUtility.PlaybackProcess.Kill();
10             LinuxPlayerUtility.PlaybackProcess.Dispose();
11             LinuxPlayerUtility.PlaybackProcess = null;
12         }
13
14         return Task.CompletedTask;
15     }
16 }
```

And its Windows-specific implementation, WindowsStopButton.cs file, will contain the following:

```
1  namespace Abstract_Factory_Demo;
2
3  internal class WindowsStopButton : StopButton
4  {
5      public override Task Stop(string fileName)
6      {
7          WindowsPlayerUtility.ExecuteMciCommand($"Stop {fi\
8  leName}");
9          return Task.CompletedTask;
10     }
11 }
```

Now, we will move on to our Abstract Factory. This will be represented by PlayerCreator.cs file, which will have the following content:

25. Abstract Factory

```
1  namespace Abstract_Factory_Demo;
2
3  internal abstract class PlayerCreator
4  {
5      public abstract PlayButton CreatePlayButton();
6      public abstract StopButton CreateStopButton();
7  }
```

So, as you can see, the **Factory** returns two objects rather than just one, as we had in the Factory Method example. Otherwise, it operates under the same principles.

We will now need to create OS-specific implementations of this **Creator** object. We will first add a Linux implementation. To do so, we will create LinuxPlayerCreator.cs file and populate it with the following content:

```
1   namespace Abstract_Factory_Demo;
2
3   internal class LinuxPlayerCreator : PlayerCreator
4   {
5       public override PlayButton CreatePlayButton()
6       {
7           return new LinuxPlayButton();
8       }
9
10      public override StopButton CreateStopButton()
11      {
12          return new LinuxStopButton();
13      }
14  }
```

Then, we will add Windows implementation by creating WindowsPlayerCreator.cs file and populating it with the following code:

```
namespace Abstract_Factory_Demo;

internal class WindowsPlayerCreator : PlayerCreator
{
    public override PlayButton CreatePlayButton()
    {
        return new WindowsPlayButton();
    }

    public override StopButton CreateStopButton()
    {
        return new WindowsStopButton();
    }
}
```

Now, we are ready to use our Abstract Factory. We will do so by replacing the content of Program.cs file with the following:

```
using Abstract_Factory_Demo;
using System.Runtime.InteropServices;

PlayerCreator? playerFactory;

if (RuntimeInformation.IsOSPlatform(OSPlatform.Windows))
    playerFactory = new WindowsPlayerCreator();
else if (RuntimeInformation.IsOSPlatform(OSPlatform.Linux\
))
    playerFactory = new LinuxPlayerCreator();
else
    throw new Exception("Only Linux and Windows operating\
 systems are supported.");

Console.WriteLine("Please specify the path to the file to\
 play.");

```

```
18  var filePath = Console.ReadLine() ?? string.Empty;
19  playerFactory.CreatePlayButton().Play(filePath);
20
21  Console.WriteLine("Playing audio. Type 'stop' to stop it \
22  or 'exit' to exit the application.");
23
24  while (true)
25  {
26      var command = Console.ReadLine();
27
28      if (command == "stop")
29          playerFactory.CreateStopButton().Stop(filePath);
30      else if (command == "exit")
31          break;
32  }
33
34  Console.ReadKey();
```

So, the code detects which operating system the application is running on and applies an OS-specific implementation of the **Factory** object. Then, calling any of the methods on the **Factory** object implementation will return OS-specific implementation of the functionality that the method is responsible for creating.

And this concludes our overview of Abstract Factory. Let's summarize what its benefits are.

Benefits of using Abstract Factory

The benefits of using Abstract Factory are the same as that of using Factory Method. Let's recap what those are:

- Abstract Factory enforces the single responsibility principle by separating conditional logic from implementation of the logic inside each condition.

- This allows us to easily maintain the code and write automated tests for it. There won't be any complex and barely readable tests assessing complex conditional logic. Instead, a couple of simple scenarios will asses that the correct implementations of **Target Objects** and **Factory** is picked up for each condition. Then, separate sets of scenarios can be applied to each separate **Target Object** and **Factory** implementation.
- Abstract Factory allows you to execute a particular condition once. Because all implementations of each **Target Object** type use a common abstraction, a concrete implementation of it can be created once and then just re-used throughout the code.

In addition to these, Abstract Factory has the following major benefit:

- Abstract Factory allows you to create a whole family of related objects in one go.

And Abstract Factory doesn't have the same caveats as Factory Method has on its own. Because you are creating a family of related objects rather than just a specific implementation of a single object, **Creator** object plays an important role and actually makes things easier.

But Abstract Factory still has some minor caveats. And this is what we will examine next.

Caveats of using Abstract Factory

Because Abstract Factory was designed to create a family of related objects in one go, it's not suitable for situations where creating an object step-by-step would be more appropriate. Builder pattern is more suitable for these types of situations. And this is what we will have a look at next.

26. Builder

Builder is a design pattern that is used for building an object in multiple steps. It's especially useful when each part of the object, rather than the entire object, needs to be built conditionally. Another situation where Builder design pattern is suitable is when you can't know ahead of time which specific part you need to add to your object.

Builder can be summarized as follows:

- There is a **Builder** class that creates a specific type of object and adds various parts to it. We will refer to the output object as **Target Object**.
- **Builder** object has various methods to modify the **Target Object** while keeping the implementation of **Target Object** inaccessible.
- **Builder** object has a method that needs to be called to produce **Target Object** once sufficient modifications have been applied to it and it's ready to be used.
- There may also be a **Director** object, which uses a specific implementation of **Builder** and is solely responsible for manipulating **Builder**. But **Director** object is not strictly required.

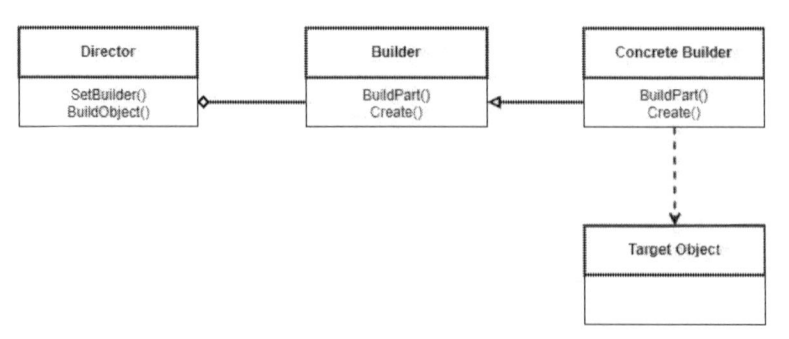

Figure 26.1 - Builder UML diagram

Perhaps one noteworthy example of a Builder design pattern implementation is StringBuilder[1] class from `System.Text` namespace of C#.

We will now go through an example implementation of Builder. The complete solution can be found via the link below:

https://github.com/fiodarsazanavets/design-patterns-in-csharp/tree/main/Creational_Patterns/Builder

Prerequisites

In order to be able to implement the code samples below, you need the following installed on your machine:

- .NET 6 SDK (or newer)
- A suitable IDE or a code editor (Visual Studio, Visual Studio Code, JetBrains Rider)

Builder implementation example

In our example, we will, once again, build an audio player that can play audios on either Linux or Windows operating system, like we

---

[1] https://docs.microsoft.com/en-us/dotnet/api/system.text.stringbuilder

did for Factory Method and Abstract Factory. But this time, we will do so by using the Builder design pattern.

We will start by creating a .NET console application. And the first thing we will do is add some static utility classes that will provide audio playback functionality on both Windows and Linux. For the Linux implementation, we will add LinuxPlayerUtility.cs file with the following content:

```csharp
using System.Diagnostics;

namespace Builder_Demo;

internal static class LinuxPlayerUtility
{
    public static Process? PlaybackProcess { get; set; }

    public static void StartBashProcess(string command)
    {
        var escapedArgs = command.Replace("\"", "\\\"");

        var process = new Process()
        {
            StartInfo = new ProcessStartInfo
            {
                FileName = "/bin/bash",
                Arguments = $"-c \"{escapedArgs}\"",
                RedirectStandardOutput = true,
                RedirectStandardInput = true,
                UseShellExecute = false,
                CreateNoWindow = true,
            }
        };

        process.Start();
    }
```

Windows implementation will be placed into `WindowsPlayerUtility.cs` file, which will contain the following code:

```
using System.Runtime.InteropServices;
using System.Text;

namespace Builder_Demo;

internal static class WindowsPlayerUtility
{
    [DllImport("winmm.dll")]
    private static extern int mciSendString(string comman\
d, StringBuilder stringReturn, int returnLength, IntPtr h\
wndCallback);

    public static void ExecuteMciCommand(string commandSt\
ring)
    {
        var sb = new StringBuilder();
        var result = mciSendString(commandString, sb, 102\
4 * 1024, IntPtr.Zero);
        Console.WriteLine(result);
    }
}
```

We will then add `PlayButton.cs` file, containing the following abstract class definition:

```
1  namespace Builder_Demo;
2
3  internal abstract class PlayButton
4  {
5      public abstract Task Play(string fileName);
6  }
```

We will then need to add an abstract class representing a Stop button. To do so, we will add StopButton.cs file with the following class definition:

```
1  namespace Builder_Demo;
2
3  internal abstract class StopButton
4  {
5      public abstract Task Stop(string fileName);
6  }
```

Both of these abstract classes will be part of a Player class, which, unlike these two abstract classes, is a concrete class. But it will still have these abstract classes as its fields. It will be a **Builder** object that will assign concrete implementations to these classes.

The player class will reside inside Player.cs file and will have the following content:

```
1  namespace Builder_Demo;
2
3  internal class Player
4  {
5      public PlayButton? PlayButton { get; set; }
6      public StopButton? StopButton { get; set; }
7  }
```

We will now need to add concrete implementations of each of the buttons. Linux implementation of the PlayButton class will be contained in LinuxPlayButton.cs file and it will be as follows:

```csharp
namespace Builder_Demo;

internal class LinuxPlayButton : PlayButton
{
    public override Task Play(string fileName)
    {
        LinuxPlayerUtility.StartBashProcess($"mpg123 -q '{fileName}'");
        return Task.CompletedTask;
    }
}
```

Windows implementation will be included in WindowsPlayButton.cs file, which will have the following content:

```csharp
namespace Builder_Demo;

internal class WindowsPlayButton : PlayButton
{
    public override Task Play(string fileName)
    {
        WindowsPlayerUtility.ExecuteMciCommand($"Play {fileName}");
        return Task.CompletedTask;
    }
}
```

Now, we will add implementations of the StopButton class. We will first add LinuxStopButton.cs file with the following content:

```
1  namespace Builder_Demo;
2
3  internal class LinuxStopButton : StopButton
4  {
5      public override Task Stop(string fileName)
6      {
7          if (LinuxPlayerUtility.PlaybackProcess != null)
8          {
9              LinuxPlayerUtility.PlaybackProcess.Kill();
10             LinuxPlayerUtility.PlaybackProcess.Dispose();
11             LinuxPlayerUtility.PlaybackProcess = null;
12         }
13
14         return Task.CompletedTask;
15     }
16 }
```

Then, we will create `WindowsStopButton.cs` file with the following code:

```
1  namespace Builder_Demo;
2
3  internal class WindowsStopButton : StopButton
4  {
5      public override Task Stop(string fileName)
6      {
7          WindowsPlayerUtility.ExecuteMciCommand($"Stop {fi\
8  leName}");
9          return Task.CompletedTask;
10     }
11 }
```

Now, we will add an interface that will allow us to build a `Player` object depending on the OS the software is running on. The interface would be added in `IPlayerBuilder.cs` file and will be as follows:

```csharp
namespace Builder_Demo;

internal interface IPlayerBuilder
{
    void AddPlayButton();
    void AddStopButton();
    Player BuildPlayer();
}
```

As you can see, there is a method for adding a Play button, a method for adding a Stop button and a method for returning a `Player` object once it has been built.

Linux implementation of this interface, which we will place in `LinuxPlayerBuilder.cs` file, will be as follows:

```csharp
namespace Builder_Demo;

internal class LinuxPlayerBuilder : IPlayerBuilder
{
    private readonly Player player = new Player();

    public void AddPlayButton()
    {
        player.PlayButton = new LinuxPlayButton();
    }

    public void AddStopButton()
    {
        player.StopButton = new LinuxStopButton();
    }

    public Player BuildPlayer()
    {
        return player;
```

```
20     }
21 }
```

For Windows implementation, we will create `WindowsPlayButton.cs` file, which will have the following content:

```
1  namespace Builder_Demo;
2
3  internal class WindowsPlayerBuilder : IPlayerBuilder
4  {
5      private readonly Player player = new Player();
6
7      public void AddPlayButton()
8      {
9          player.PlayButton = new WindowsPlayButton();
10     }
11
12     public void AddStopButton()
13     {
14         player.StopButton = new WindowsStopButton();
15     }
16
17     public Player BuildPlayer()
18     {
19         return player;
20     }
21 }
```

And then we will also add a **Director** object. It will go into `PlayerDirector.cs` file and its definition will be as follows:

```
namespace Builder_Demo;

internal class PlayerDirector
{
    public Player BuildPlayer(IPlayerBuilder builder)
    {
        builder.AddPlayButton();
        builder.AddStopButton();
        return builder.BuildPlayer();
    }
}
```

Basically, the **Director** object accepts a specific implementation of `IPlayerInterface` and calls all sequential steps on it to build a `Player` object.

Let's now add the actual application logic. We will do so by replacing the content of `Program.cs` file with the following:

```
using Builder_Demo;
using System.Runtime.InteropServices;

var director = new PlayerDirector();
Player? player;

if (RuntimeInformation.IsOSPlatform(OSPlatform.Windows))
    player = director.BuildPlayer(new WindowsPlayerBuilde\
r());
else if (RuntimeInformation.IsOSPlatform(OSPlatform.Linux\
))
    player = director.BuildPlayer(new LinuxPlayerBuilder(\
));
else
    throw new Exception("Only Linux and Windows operating\
 systems are supported.");
```

```
18   Console.WriteLine("Please specify the path to the file to\
19    play.");
20
21   var filePath = Console.ReadLine() ?? string.Empty;
22   player.PlayButton?.Play(filePath);
23
24   Console.WriteLine("Playing audio. Type 'stop' to stop it \
25   or 'exit' to exit the application.");
26
27   while (true)
28   {
29       var command = Console.ReadLine();
30
31       if (command == "stop")
32           player.StopButton?.Stop(filePath);
33       else if (command == "exit")
34           break;
35   }
36
37   Console.ReadKey();
```

What we do here is detect which operating system we are on. And then, depending on the host OS, we pass a specific implementation of our **Builder** object into the **Director**. This, in turn, will build an OS-specific implementation of Player object.

This concludes our overview of the Builder design pattern. Let's summarize what its benefits are.

Benefits of using Builder

The core benefits of using Builder can be summarized as follows:

- Builder allows you to build an object step by step, which reduces complexity in the code and enforces single respon-

sibility principle.
- This allows us to easily maintain the code and write automated tests for it. As each method in a **Builder** object plays a very specific role, it's easy to come up with test cases for it.
- If **Director** object is applied, Builder design pattern allows you to build different representations of the same object.

However, Builder design pattern comes with an important caveat that developers need to be aware of.

Caveats of using Builder

Both our Abstract Factory and Builder examples produced a solution that is identical in functionality from the user's perspective. However, if you have a look at the code, you will notice how much more complex Builder implementation is. And this is the main disadvantage of using Builder. It increases the complexity of your code.

This is why, unless you need to build an object step-by-step, Abstract Factory would be a better choice than Builder. If you can create an entire object in one go, you aren't really getting any advantage from using Builder. But you are paying an additional price by making your code more complex.

27. Prototype

Prototype is a design pattern that allows you to easily clone existing objects. Instead of copying all the data from one object to another field-by-field, you just have a method to clone the object inside the object itself.

This has two core advantages. Firstly, all of your code of copying an object resides in a single place in your code base, which enforces *don't repeat yourself* (DRY) principle. Secondly, it allows you to copy private fields into the new object, which you wouldn't have been able to do at all if you just did a field-by-field copying.

Prototype can be summarized as follows:

- A class has a method that returns an exact copy of the instance of the class.
- This method may be called `Clone` or `Copy`.
- This method performs field-by-field copy of the class, including its private fields.
- But even though the object that this method returns has the same values in all of its fields as the original object, it's a completely different object reference, so modifying it will not change the original object.

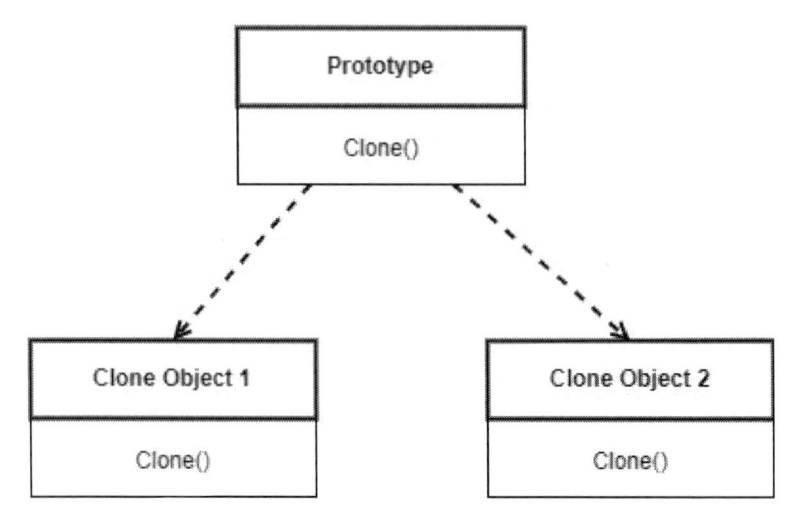

Figure 27.1 - **Prototype UML diagram**

We will now go through an example implementation of Prototype. The complete solution can be found via the link below:

https://github.com/fiodarsazanavets/design-patterns-in-csharp/tree/main/Creational_Patterns/Prototype

Prerequisites

In order to be able to implement the code samples below, you need the following installed on your machine:

- .NET 6 SDK (or newer)
- A suitable IDE or a code editor (Visual Studio, Visual Studio Code, JetBrains Rider)

Prototype implementation example

To demonstrate Prototype design pattern, we will create a .NET console application project.

When using Prototype, it would be a good practice to create an interface that you would want any cloneable class to implement. This will make all cloneable types behave consistently. So, we will add ICloneable.cs file with the following interface definition:

```
namespace Prototype_Demo;

internal interface ICloneable
{
    ICloneable Clone();
}
```

Then, we will create the actual cloneable object. It will be added as CloneableObject.cs file and its code will be as follows:

```
namespace Prototype_Demo;

internal class CloneableObject : ICloneable
{
    private readonly int internalData;
    private readonly string internalTitle;

    public CloneableObject(string title)
    {
        var random = new Random();
        internalData = random.Next();

        internalTitle = title;
    }

```

```
16      public int Data => internalData;
17      public string Title => internalTitle;
18
19      public ICloneable Clone()
20      {
21          return (CloneableObject)MemberwiseClone();
22      }
23  }
```

So, in our class, we have two public readonly properties: Data and Title. None of them can be changed once the object has been created. But we have the Clone method that returns a copy of our object by calling the MemberwiseClone method of the base object data type. This method will perform field-by-field copying of our object. And this will include the private fields.

Let's now see if our Clone method behaves as we have intended. To do so, we will replace the content of Program.cs file with the following:

```
1   using Prototype_Demo;
2
3   var object1 = new CloneableObject("Title 1");
4
5   Console.WriteLine($"Object 1 title: {object1.Title}");
6   Console.WriteLine($"Object 1 data: {object1.Data}");
7
8   var object2 = (CloneableObject)object1.Clone();
9
10  Console.WriteLine($"Object 2 title: {object2.Title}");
11  Console.WriteLine($"Object 2 data: {object2.Data}");
12
13  Console.ReadKey();
```

In here, we create an object and give it a specific title. Its Data property will be populated with a random integer when the object is created. We output both the Title and Data properties into the console. Then we create another instance of this object by cloning our initial object instance. And we, once again, output its Title and Data properties into the console to verify that they have the same values as in our first object.

And, as this figure demonstrates, the values of the properties are the same. This proves that the cloning process works.

```
Object 1 title: Title 1
Object 1 data: 730785888
Object 2 title: Title 1
Object 2 data: 730785888
```

Figure 27.2 - **Proof that our object cloning works**

This concludes our overview of the Prototype design pattern. Let's now go through the summary of its main benefits.

Benefits of using Prototype

The main benefits of using the Prototype design pattern can be summarized as follows:

- If you need to copy an object, the logic of copying it will be present in a single place in the entire codebase, which enforces DRY principle.
- Because cloning of an object is performed inside the object itself, private fields can be copied too.

Let's now have a look at caveats that you need to be familiar with while using the Prototype design pattern (although there aren't many of them).

Caveats of using Prototype

One thing that you need to be aware of while using Prototype is the difference between shallow and deep copying. When you perform a shallow copy, which is exactly what we had a look at in our example, only the values of the fields with basic data types get copied. So, the fields containing `string`, `int`, `double`, `bool`, etc. will be copied, but the fields containing custom data types, such as classes, won't be.

Deep copy is when you copy everything, including any custom data types that your object contains and any custom data type fields that those custom data types contain. Therefore, to ensure that you can perform a deep copy, you need to either make the other data types cloneable or perform manual field-by-field copying inside of your `Clone` method.

Other than that, there are no caveats of using Prototype design pattern. It is the best way to copy objects.

28. Singleton

Singleton design pattern allows you to use a single instance of a particular object throughout your application. This is achieved with the help of a private constructor and a static method that can call this constructor from the outside.

Singleton can be summarized as follows:

- A **Singleton** class that is meant to be used as a single instance that is shared throughout an application has a private constructor, so it can only be created inside of the class itself.
- The class holds a private static field containing its own data type.
- To instantiate the class from the outside, the class has a static method that returns the same data type as the class itself.
- This method will create an instance of the class via the private constructor and populate the private static field with this instance. Then this instance would be returned to the caller.
- Any subsequent calls will just return the object instance that was already created.

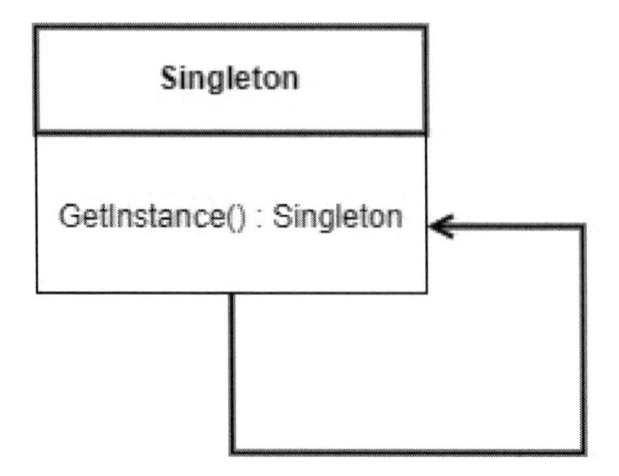

Figure 28.1 - Singleton UML diagram

We will now go through an example implementation of Singleton. The complete solution can be found via the link below:

https://github.com/fiodarsazanavets/design-patterns-in-csharp/tree/main/Creational_Patterns/Singleton

Prerequisites

In order to be able to implement the code samples below, you need the following installed on your machine:

- .NET 6 SDK (or newer)
- A suitable IDE or a code editor (Visual Studio, Visual Studio Code, JetBrains Rider)

Singleton implementation example

We will create a .NET console application and add a **Singleton** class to it. For this purpose, we will add SingletonObject.cs file with the following content:

```csharp
namespace Singleton_Demo;

internal class SingletonObject
{
    private static SingletonObject? instance;

    public static SingletonObject GetInstance()
    {
        if (instance is null)
        {
            var random = new Random();
            instance = new SingletonObject(random.Next());
        }

        return instance;
    }

    private SingletonObject(int data)
    {
        Data = data;
    }

    public int Data { get; private set; }
}
```

So, as you can see, we have a private constructor and a private static instance field with the same data type as the class itself. Then there is a static GetInstance method, which creates a new instance of the object on the first call and then just reuses it in every subsequent call.

Because it's a static method, it will behave exactly the same, regardless where in the application it's called from. And this means that the object instance that it will return will also be the same.

Now, we will replace the content of Program.cs file with the following:

```
using Singleton_Demo;

var object1 = SingletonObject.GetInstance();
Console.WriteLine($"Data of object 1: {object1.Data}");

var object2 = SingletonObject.GetInstance();
Console.WriteLine($"Data of object 2: {object2.Data}");

Console.WriteLine($"Are objects equal? {object.Equals(obj\
ect1, object2)}");

Console.ReadKey();
```

So, essentially, we are verifying whether the same instance of an object gets returned every time we call GetInstance method on the **Singleton** object. And, as the console output demonstrates, it does indeed return the same instance of the object:

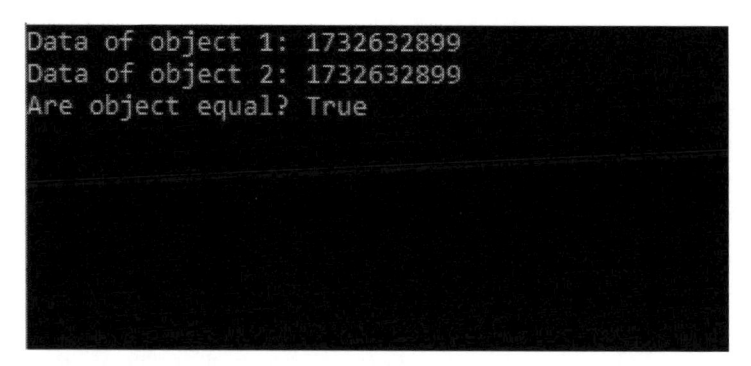

```
Data of object 1: 1732632899
Data of object 2: 1732632899
Are object equal? True
```

Figure 28.2 - Singleton object returns the same instance of itself

And this concludes the overview of Singleton design pattern. Let's now summarize its key benefits.

Benefits of using Singleton

The key benefits of using Singleton are as follows:

- The object is only initialized once - the first time you retrieve it.
- The design pattern enforces the use of the same instance of the object throughout the application.
- The design pattern is easy to understand and set up.

However, just like any other design pattern, Singleton has its caveats. And this is what we will have a look at next.

Caveats of using Singleton

Arguably, Singleton design pattern violates the single responsibility principle, as the **Singleton** object is responsible for both maintaining an instance of itself and performing the actual functionality the object was designed for.

Another disadvantage of using Singleton is that it may not behave as intended in a multi-threaded application. It could be that each thread would create its own instance of a **Singleton** object.

Also, **Singleton** object isn't necessarily the easiest object type to write tests against. Especially, it will be difficult to mock, as static methods cannot be mocked by conventional means.

Finally, there is no flexibility in how the object is used. A **Singleton** object can only ever be used as **Singleton**. It cannot be used as an instance per dependency under a different context.

But all of these problems can easily be solved. The classic Singleton design pattern, as demonstrated here, has been superseded by dependency injection. Any dependency injection framework, whether it's inbuilt ASP.NET Core system or a third-party framework, such as Autofac or Ninject, allows you to register absolutely any object as **Singleton**. And then, this object will be simply injected into the constructor of any class that depends on it.

For example, if we were to use the standard dependency injection mechanism in ASP.NET Core, all we need to do is add the following line in our Program.cs file before the application is built:

```
services.AddSingleton<Interface, Implementation>();
```

In this context, Interface represents an interface that is used as constructor parameter. Implementation represents a concrete class that implement this interface that will actually be injected into the constructors. It is an example of dependency inversion principle that was described in **chapter 5**.

This way, you will be able to easily mock your objects, so writing tests becomes easy. You no longer have to maintain private constructors and static methods, so you can maintain single responsibility principle. Also, this allows you to have this object type as a non-singleton object in other contexts. Finally, regestring a dependency as a singleton will guarantee that you will use the same instance of the object even in a multi-threaded environment.

Structural design patterns

Structural design patterns prescribe how to structure your objects. This section covers the following patterns:

- Adapter
- Bridge
- Composite
- Decorator
- Facade
- Flyweight
- Proxy

29. Adapter

Adapter design pattern is used when you need to access some endpoint that is not compatible with the rest of your application, but you have no means of changing the endpoint. It has many real-life analogies.

Different regions of the world have different electric sockets. For example, a socket somewhere in continental Europe works with a plug that has two pins, while a British socket works with a triple-pin plug. So, if you bought some electric appliance in Britain and then traveled to continental Europe with it, you won't be able to plug it directly into a socket. You will need to get a socket adapter. This adapter will have two pins, which will allow it to be connected to a European socket, but it will also have a socket of its own, which will accept a British plug.

Adapter can be summarized as follows:

- There is a service that is routinely accessed by an application (we will call it **Service Implementation**).
- This service implements some interface (which we will call **Service Interface**).
- There is an endpoint that needs to be accessed by the same part of the application that isn't compatible with the **Service Interface**.
- To solve this problem, there is an **Adapter** class, which implements the **Service Interface**, but has some internal translation functionality to be able to access this incompatible endpoint.

29. Adapter

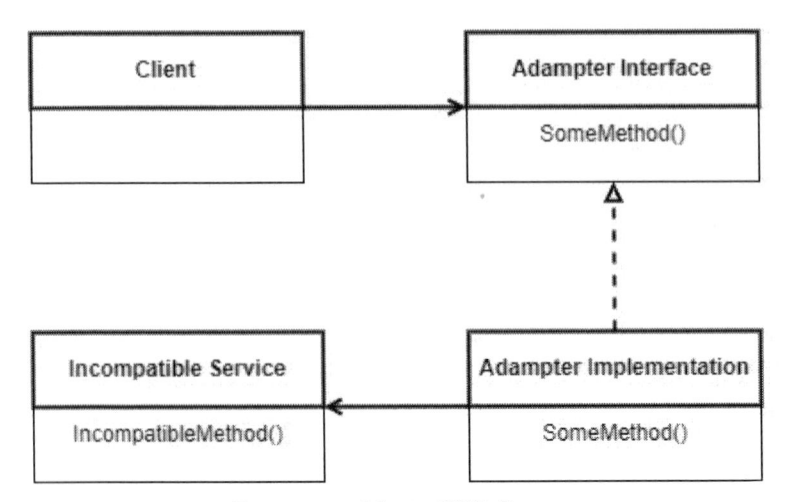

Figure 29.1 - Adapter UML diagram

For example, your application might be dealing with JSON data, but there's still an endpoint that deals with XML. And this endpoint cannot be changed, as many other services depend on it. So, if you want to be able to use this endpoint in the JSON-based part of your application, you need an **Adapter** that will translate between XML and JSON.

We will now go through an example implementation of Adapter. The complete solution can be found via the link below:

https://github.com/fiodarsazanavets/design-patterns-in-csharp/tree/main/Structural_Patterns/Adapter

Prerequisites

In order to be able to implement the code samples below, you need the following installed on your machine:

- .NET 6 SDK (or newer)
- A suitable IDE or a code editor (Visual Studio, Visual Studio Code, JetBrains Rider)

Adapter implementation example

In this example, we will use the concept of electric sockets. We will mimic the use of a socket adapter in the code.

We will create a standard .NET console application. Then, we will add the IElectricSocket.cs file to it. The file will contain the following empty interface definition:

```
1  namespace Adapter_Demo;
2
3  internal interface IElectricSocket
4  {
5  }
```

Then, we will create an interface representing a socket plug. For this, we will add ISocketPlug.cs file with the following content:

```
1  namespace Adapter_Demo;
2
3  internal interface ISocketPlug
4  {
5      void SelectSocket(IElectricSocket socket);
6      void ConnectToSocket();
7  }
```

After this, we will need to add a specific interface that will allow us to connect to a European electric socket. This interface will inherit from IElectricSocket and will look like this:

```
1  namespace Adapter_Demo;
2
3  internal interface IEuropeanElectricSocket : IElectricSoc\
4  ket
5  {
6      void ConnectTwoPins();
7  }
```

The main implementation of our interface will look like this:

```
1  namespace Adapter_Demo;
2
3  internal class EuropeanElectricSocket : IEuropeanElectric\
4  Socket
5  {
6      public void ConnectTwoPins()
7      {
8          Console.WriteLine("Double-pin plug has been succe\
9  ssfully connected.");
10     }
11 }
```

We will also have an interface and implementation for a British electric socket:

```
1  namespace Adapter_Demo;
2
3  internal interface IBritishElectricSocket : IElectricSock\
4  et
5  {
6      void ConnectThreePins();
7  }
8
9  internal class BritishElectricSocket : IBritishElectricSo\
10 cket
```

```
11  {
12      public void ConnectThreePins()
13      {
14          Console.WriteLine("Triple-pin plug has been succe\
15  ssfully connected.");
16      }
17  }
```

As you can see, even though it's still an electric socket, you can't connect a plug with two pins to it. You need three pins.

But the definition of our class that represents European socket plug will look as follows:

```
1   namespace Adapter_Demo;
2
3   internal class EuropeanSocketPlug : ISocketPlug
4   {
5       private IEuropeanElectricSocket? europeanSocket;
6
7       public void ConnectToSocket()
8       {
9           europeanSocket?.ConnectTwoPins();
10      }
11
12      public void SelectSocket(IElectricSocket socket)
13      {
14          if (socket is not IEuropeanElectricSocket)
15          {
16              throw new ArgumentException("The European plu\
17  g can only be connected to a European socket.");
18          }
19
20          europeanSocket = (IEuropeanElectricSocket)socket;
21      }
22  }
```

As you can see, it can only work with classes that implement IEuropeanElectricSocket. IBritishElectricSocket implementations will not be compatible with it. And this is where we would need our adapter.

In our case, IEuropeanElectricSocket and IBritishElectricSocket are **Service Interfaces**, while EuropeanElectricSocket and BritishElectricSocket are **Service Implementations**. However, they represent different services that aren't compatible with one another. To solve this problem, we will need to add an **Adapter** object, which will represent another **Service Implementations** of IEuropeanElectricSocket interface, but internally will be able to work with IBritishElectricSocket implementations. And this is what our **Adapter** will look like:

```
namespace Adapter_Demo
{
    internal class SocketAdapter : IEuropeanElectricSocke\
t, ISocketPlug
    {
        private IBritishElectricSocket? britishSocket;

        public void ConnectToSocket()
        {
            britishSocket?.ConnectThreePins();
        }

        public void ConnectTwoPins()
        {
            Console.WriteLine("Double-pin plug has been s\
uccessfully connected to the adapter.");
        }

        public void SelectSocket(IElectricSocket socket)
        {
            if (socket is not IBritishElectricSocket)
```

```
22              {
23                  throw new ArgumentException("The adapter \
24 can only be connected to a British socket.");
25              }
26
27              britishSocket = (IBritishElectricSocket) sock\
28 et;
29          }
30      }
31 }
```

In our case, the **Adapter** acts both as ISocketPlug and IEuropeanElectricSocket, just like a real-life socket adapter would. It has the ConnectTwoPins method, which allows it to be used by an instance of the EuropeanSocketPlug class. But it also has SelectSocket and ConnectToSocket methods, which allows it to be connected to another socket. And this time, the socket it can connect to is an implementation of IBritishElectricSocket interface.

Let's now see how this adapter works. To do so, we will replace the content of Program.cs file with the following:

```
1  using Adapter_Demo;
2
3  var socketPlug = new EuropeanSocketPlug();
4  socketPlug.SelectSocket(new EuropeanElectricSocket());
5  socketPlug.ConnectToSocket();
6
7  var adapter = new SocketAdapter();
8  adapter.SelectSocket(new BritishElectricSocket());
9  adapter.ConnectToSocket();
10
11 socketPlug.SelectSocket(adapter);
12 socketPlug.ConnectToSocket();
```

```
13
14  Console.ReadKey();
```

So, we are first connecting a European socket plug into a European socket. Then we are connecting a socket adapter into a British socket. Finally, we are connecting the European socket plug into the adapter. And this is what we get as the output if we run the application:

```
Double-pin plug has been successfully connected.
Triple-pin plug has been successfully connected.
Double-pin plug has been successfully connected to the adapter.
```

Figure 29.2 - Demonstration of adapter use

This concludes our overview of Adapter. Let's summarize its main benefits.

Benefits of using Adapter

Adapter design pattern has the following benefits:

- It allows you to make your application work with incompatible services without changing overall application logic.
- Any translation between an incompatible API and the rest of the application are confined to a single place, which makes the code easy to maintain.
- It works well when an incompatible API cannot be changed for any reason (it's maintained by a third party, many other services depend on it, etc.).

But, just like any other design pattern, Adapter has its caveats.

Caveats of using Adapter

Perhaps the main disadvantage of using Adapter is that it makes code more complicated. You need to add a suitable **Service Interface**, which may have to be more complex to make it work with an **Adapter** object. Also, translation functionality itself may have to be very complex. Yes, the above example is fairly trivial. But in a real-life situation, you may have to do some truly complex data transformation inside an **Adapter** object.

This is why, if you can, it's better to just change the incompatible service and make it compatible instead of using Adapter design pattern. Use Adapter only if the service that you need to access is either a third-party service that cannot be changed, or if too many other components depend on the existing API, which makes it too expensive to change.

30. Bridge

Bridge design pattern allows you to separate the business logic from a software component that controls or triggers this business logic. For example, you may have a user interface that has multiple buttons. Each of these buttons triggers some logic in the back-end. Bridge design pattern allows you to separate the user face with the buttons from the component that contains the actual business logic.

The main benefit of using the Bridge design pattern would be that it allows two separate teams to work independently on two application components. One team would be responsible for the user interface and the other team would be responsible for the implementation of the business logic in the back-end. The teams can work independently as long as they have specified a shared interface definition.

Bridge can be summarized as follows:

- There are two objects: **Interface** and **Implementation**. They are not to be confused with interfaces and classes. In this context, the object playing the role of **Interface** is actually a concrete class.
- **Implementation** object contains the main business logic, while **Interface** object is design to interact with all endpoints of **Implementation** object.
- **Implementation** object depends on an interface (in the normal sense of object-oriented programming), so it can be easily mocked when **Interface** object needs to be tested.

30. Bridge

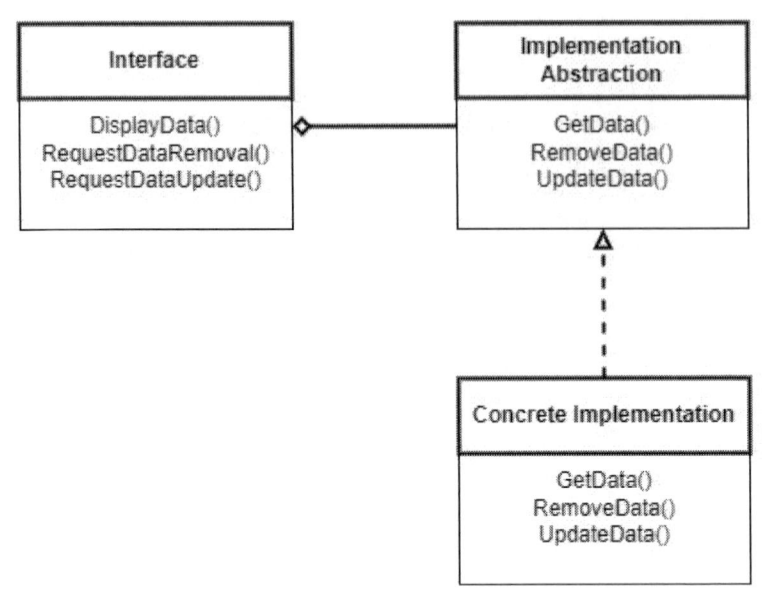

```
┌─────────────────────────┐         ┌─────────────────────────┐
│        Interface        │         │     Implementation      │
│                         │         │      Abstraction        │
├─────────────────────────┤◇────────├─────────────────────────┤
│ DisplayData()           │         │ GetData()               │
│ RequestDataRemoval()    │         │ RemoveData()            │
│ RequestDataUpdate()     │         │ UpdateData()            │
└─────────────────────────┘         └─────────────────────────┘
                                                 △
                                                 ┊
                                                 ┊
                                    ┌─────────────────────────┐
                                    │  Concrete Implementation│
                                    ├─────────────────────────┤
                                    │ GetData()               │
                                    │ RemoveData()            │
                                    │ UpdateData()            │
                                    └─────────────────────────┘
```

Figure 30.1 - Bridge UML diagram

We will now go through an example implementation of Bridge. The complete solution can be found via the link below:

https://github.com/fiodarsazanavets/design-patterns-in-csharp/tree/main/Structural_Patterns/Bridge

Prerequisites

In order to be able to implement the code samples below, you need the following installed on your machine:

- .NET 6 SDK (or newer)
- A suitable IDE or a code editor (Visual Studio, Visual Studio Code, JetBrains Rider)

Bridge implementation example

Bridge works best if we use the **Implementation** and the **Interface** objects in separate libraries. This allows separate teams to work on separate components without affecting each other's code base. And this is what we will do in our example.

For our **Implementation** object, we will create a .NET class library and we will call it BridgeImplementation. We will then add the following IDataService.cs file to the project folder of the class library. The file will have the following content:

```
namespace BridgeImplementation;

public interface IDataService
{
    List<string> GetData();
    void InsertData(string item);
}
```

Let's imagine that there's some service that returns some data from a database. This interface represents the access points of such a service. We can retrieve the data by calling the GetData method and we can insert new items by calling the InsertData method.

For demonstration purposes, we won't be calling any database queries. We would merely work with an in-memory collection. So the representation of our **Implementation** object will be as follows:

```
namespace BridgeImplementation;

public class DataService : IDataService
{
    private readonly List<string> data;

    public DataService()
    {
        data = new();
    }

    public List<string> GetData()
    {
        return data;
    }

    public void InsertData(string item)
    {
        data.Add(item);
    }
}
```

And now we will define our **Interface** object. To do so, we will create a .NET console application and a reference to our `BridgeImplementation` from it. Our **Interface** object will be represented by `BridgeInterface.cs` file, which will have the following content:

```csharp
global using BridgeImplementation;

namespace Bridge_Demo;

internal class BridgeInterface
{
    public IDataService? Implementation { get; set; }

    public void GetData()
    {
        if (Implementation is null)
        {
            Console.WriteLine("No data.");
            return;
        }

        foreach (var item in Implementation.GetData())
        {
            Console.WriteLine(item);
        }
    }

    public void InsertData(string item)
    {
        Implementation?.InsertData(item);
    }
}
```

So, for each of the public methods on the **Implementation** object, the **Interface** object has a method of its own. The role of each of these method inside the **Interface** object is to control the **Implementation** and display the data that was returned from the **Implementation**.

In our case, we are outputting data into the console. But you can imagine how a similar principle can be used to output the data into a graphical user interface.

Please note that our **Interface** object depends on an interface that the **Implementation** object implements. It won't be a good idea to use the concrete implementation. Firstly, it would violate the dependency inversion principle. Secondly, using an interface would allow you to assign both the concrete implementation of it and a mock implementation that you can use for testing.

Finally, we will replace the content of our `Program.cs` class with the following:

```
using Bridge_Demo;

var bridgeInterface = new BridgeInterface();
bridgeInterface.Implementation = new DataService();

Console.WriteLine("Inserting item 1 into data service");
bridgeInterface.InsertData("item 1");
Console.WriteLine("Inserting item 2 into data service");
bridgeInterface.InsertData("item 2");
Console.WriteLine("Inserting item 3 into data service");
bridgeInterface.InsertData("item 3");

Console.WriteLine("Retrieving data from the service:");
bridgeInterface.GetData();

Console.ReadLine();
```

In here, we are inserting some data into the data service and then retrieving it via the **Interface** object. And, as we can see from the following output, we get the data displayed in the console:

```
Inserting item 1 into data service
Inserting item 2 into data service
Inserting item 3 into data service
Retrieving data from the service:
item 1
item 2
item 3
```

Figure 30.2 - Interface displays data that was retrieved from Implementation

This concludes the overview of the Bridge design pattern. Let's now summarize its benefits.

Benefits of using Bridge

The benefits of using Bridge design pattern can be summarized as follows:

- The main benefit of separating **Interface** from **Implementation** is that separate teams can work on these two components without interfering with each other.
- Because of such structure, it enforces the single responsibility principle.
- **Interface** can easily be tested even when **Implementation** is not ready. Due to dependency inversion principle, **Implementation** can be easily mocked.

Let's now have a look at the caveats of using Bridge.

Caveats of using Bridge

Although Bridge is a very useful design pattern, the classic version of it is rarely used these days. But it's not because of its ineffectiveness. It's because Bridge has inspired the creation of some other design patterns, such as Model-View-Controller (MVC) and Model-View-ViewModel (MVVM). These design patterns are very similar to Bridge, but are more context-specific. Therefore it makes them more useful in many situations than classic Bridge.

The principles of Bridge design pattern have also inspired architectural best practices of distributed software. For example, gRPC is, pretty much, a distributed implementation of the Bridge design pattern. Protobuf definitions that clients and servers share can be thought of as the shared Bridge interface. In this context, a gRPC client can be thought of as an **Interface** object and a server-side gRPC service can be considered to be an **Implementation**.

So, even if you don't intend to use Bridge in its classic form, it's still worth being familiar with it to understand the good practices of modern software architecture.

31. Composite

Composite design pattern allows you to efficiently create tree-like structures. This ability can be useful in many situations. For example, if you need to write software that manages the file system of a computer, you would want to be able to create folders and files. Also, every folder may contain zero or more other folders. And this is what makes a file system a good example of a tree-like structure that the Composite design pattern was intended to create.

Composite can be summarized as follows:

- There is a **Leaf** object, which cannot contain other objects.
- There is a **Composite** object, which may contain either **Leaf** objects or other **Composite** objects.
- There is a **Component** interface that both the **Composite** and the **Leaf** objects implement.
- The children of a **Composite** object are of the **Component** type, which makes it possible to add either **Leaf** or **Composite** objects to it.
- It is relatively easy to navigate through the object hierarchy and manipulate it.

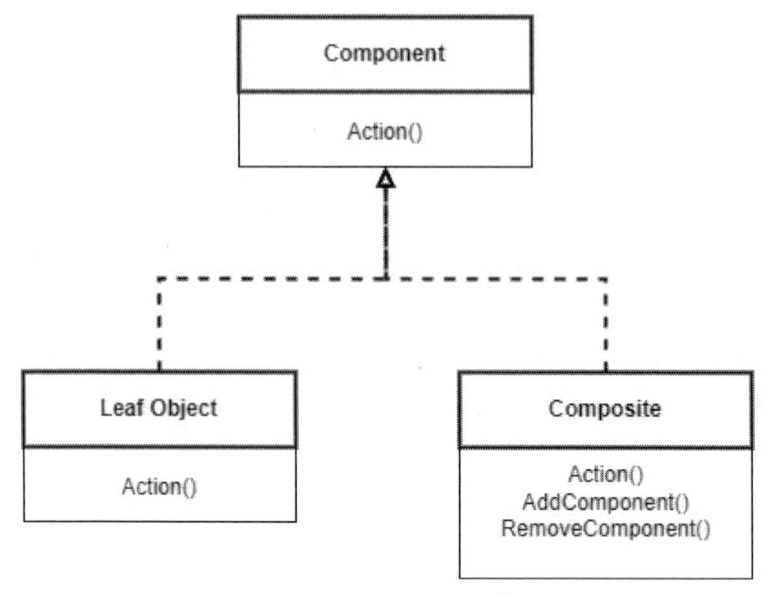

Figure 31.1 - Composite UML diagram

So, if we would use the file system as an example, a folder would be a **Composite** object, while a file would be a **Leaf** object.

We will now go through an example implementation of Composite. The complete solution can be found via the link below:

https://github.com/fiodarsazanavets/design-patterns-in-csharp/tree/main/Structural_Patterns/Composite

Prerequisites

In order to be able to implement the code samples below, you need the following installed on your machine:

- .NET 6 SDK (or newer)
- A suitable IDE or a code editor (Visual Studio, Visual Studio Code, JetBrains Rider)

Composite implementation example

Because a file system is a good representation of a tree-like hierarchy that Composite design pattern can build, we will use an abstract representation of a file system in our code.

We will create a .NET console application and add IComponent.cs file to it, which will contain the following interface:

```
namespace Composite_Demo;

internal interface IComponent
{
    string Name { get; }
    void Display(string currentPath);
}
```

Basically, the interface contains the common functionality for both a file and a folder. Each of those has a name. And each of those can be displayed.

Then we will add File.cs file with the following class definition:

```
namespace Composite_Demo;

internal class File : IComponent
{
    public File(string name)
    {
        Name = name;
    }

    public string Name { get; }

    public void Display(string currentPath)
```

```
13      {
14          Console.WriteLine(currentPath + Name);
15      }
16  }
```

Not much here. A file has a name. And it can display its own name by appending it at the end of the path that it receives.

Now, we will add a representation of a folder. It will go into Folder.cs file, which will have the following content:

```
1   namespace Composite_Demo;
2
3   internal class Folder : IComponent
4   {
5       private readonly List<IComponent> children;
6
7       public Folder(string name)
8       {
9           Name = name;
10          children = new();
11      }
12
13      public string Name { get; }
14
15      public void Display(string currentPath)
16      {
17          Console.WriteLine(currentPath + Name +
18              Path.DirectorySeparatorChar);
19      }
20
21      public void Add(IComponent child)
22      {
23          children.Add(child);
24      }
25
```

```
26        public void Remove(string name)
27        {
28            var childToRemove = children.FirstOrDefault(c => \
29   c.Name == name);
30
31            if (childToRemove is not null)
32                children.Remove(childToRemove);
33        }
34
35        public void DisplayChildren(string path)
36        {
37            foreach (var item in children)
38            {
39                item.Display(path + Name +
40                    Path.DirectorySeparatorChar);
41
42                if (item is Folder folder)
43                {
44                    folder.DisplayChildren(path + Name +
45                        Path.DirectorySeparatorChar);
46                }
47            }
48        }
49   }
```

So, this is our **Composite** object. It can display its name. But it also contains functionality for adding, removing and displaying children.

Let's now see this implementation of Composite design pattern in action. For this, we will replace the content of Program.cs file with the following:

```
using Composite_Demo;

var rootFolder = new Folder("Root");
rootFolder.Add(new Folder("Folder1"));
rootFolder.Add(new Folder("Folder2"));

var complexFolder = new Folder("Folder3");
complexFolder.Add(new Folder("Folder4"));
complexFolder.Add(new Composite_Demo.File("NewFile.xml"));
complexFolder.Add(new Composite_Demo.File("NewFile2.xml")\
);

rootFolder.Add(complexFolder);

rootFolder.DisplayChildren(string.Empty);

Console.ReadKey();
```

This logic creates and displays a bunch of files and folders. The output of it would look like this:

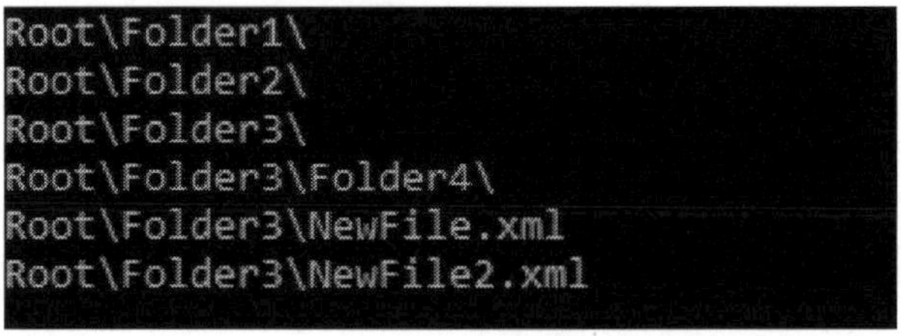

```
Root\Folder1\
Root\Folder2\
Root\Folder3\
Root\Folder3\Folder4\
Root\Folder3\NewFile.xml
Root\Folder3\NewFile2.xml
```

Figure 31.2 - Displaying hierarchy generated by Composite design pattern

Let's now summarize the main benefits of using the Composite design pattern.

Benefits of using Composite

The main benefits of using the Composite can be summarized as follows:

- Composite design pattern is by far the best way of working with complex tree-like structures.
- The design pattern helps to enforce the open-closed principle. You can add new object types into the hierarchy without modifying any existing ones.

But, just like any other design patterns, Composite comes with some caveats.

Caveats of using Composite

There aren't really many disadvantages of using the Composite design pattern. Perhaps the only disadvantage is that, when you have to deal with many object types, it may become harder to maintain all the interfaces.

As you have seen in the above example, **Leaf** and **Composite** objects are different. Even though they share a common **Component** interface, a **Composite** will always have some functionality that a **Leaf** cannot have, while a **Leaf** may also have some functionality that a **Composite** cannot have. But you may also have many different types of **Leaf** and **Composite** objects.

This is just something to be aware of. Other than that, there is no better way to build complex hierarchies than the Composite design pattern.

32. Decorator

Decorator design pattern allows developers to modify the functionality of existing objects without modifying the objects themselves. Just like Adapter pattern, Decorator provides a wrapper for an existing object. However, unlike Adapter, it implements exactly the same interface as the original object. This allows you to apply additional processing steps to the original API without modifying its original behavior.

Decorator can be summarized as follows:

- There is a class, which we will refer to as the **Original Object**.
- The **Original Object** implements **Service Interface**.
- There is a **Decorator** class that also implements **Service Interface**.
- Because **Decorator** class acts as a wrapper for **Service Interface**, any implementation of this **Service Interface** can be used, including another **Decorator**.
- **Decorator** can add additional functionality to any public members of its internal **Service Interface** implementation, such as pre-processing or post-processing steps.

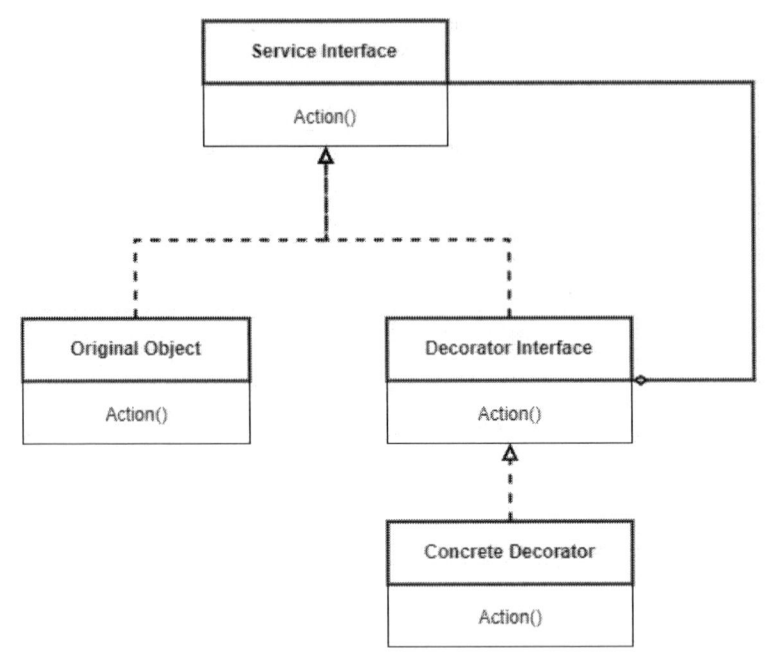

Figure 32.1 - **Decorator UML diagram**

We will now go through an example implementation of Decorator. The complete solution can be found via the link below:

https://github.com/fiodarsazanavets/design-patterns-in-csharp/tree/main/Structural_Patterns/Decorator

Prerequisites

In order to be able to implement the code samples below, you need the following installed on your machine:

- .NET 6 SDK (or newer)
- A suitable IDE or a code editor (Visual Studio, Visual Studio Code, JetBrains Rider)

Decorator implementation example

One real-life analogy of Decorator would be a gun that can have a silencer attached to it. Silencer doesn't change its base functionality of shooting bullets. But it changes the level of noise that the shots generate. And this is what we will use in the code as an abstraction.

We will create a .NET console application. Once created, we will add IGun interface to it, which will be the **Service Interface** used by both our gun object (the **Original Object**) and all of its **Decorators**. The interface will look like this:

```
namespace Decorator_Demo;

internal interface IGun
{
    bool Shoot();
    void Reload();
}
```

We can shoot the gun and we can reload it. If the gun fails to make a shot (e.g. if it's out of ammo), the Shoot method returns false. Otherwise it returns true.

And this is what the implementation of our **Original Object** looks like:

```csharp
namespace Decorator_Demo;

internal class Gun : IGun
{
    private int ammo = 0;

    public void Reload()
    {
        ammo = 6;
    }

    public bool Shoot()
    {
        if (ammo > 0)
        {
            Console.WriteLine("Shot fired.");
            ammo--;
            return true;
        }

        Console.WriteLine("Out of ammo.");
        return false;
    }
}
```

So, we have an integer that represents how much ammo we have left. Every time we reload, the integer gets reset to 6. Every time we shoot, the ammo gets decremented by one. And if there was any ammo at the beginning of the shot, `true` is returned. Otherwise, if the ammo counter was zero, `false` is returned. In either situation, the outcome is printed in the console.

Now we will start adding some **Decorator** objects. To demonstrate how multiple decorators can be applied, we will create two of them. And to help us with this, we will create an abstract class that both of them will implement. This class will look as follows:

```csharp
namespace Decorator_Demo;

internal abstract class GunDecorator : IGun
{
    private IGun? gun;

    public void SetGun(IGun gun)
    {
        this.gun = gun;
    }

    public virtual void Reload()
    {
        if (gun is not null)
        {
            gun.Reload();
        }
    }

    public virtual bool Shoot()
    {
        if (gun is not null)
        {
            return gun.Shoot();
        }

        return false;
    }
}
```

As you can see, the base **Decorator** class implements the same **Service Interface** as our **Original Object**. Now, we will add some implementations to it. First, we will add Silencer class, which will look as follows:

```
namespace Decorator_Demo;

internal class Silencer : GunDecorator
{
    public override bool Shoot()
    {
        if (base.Shoot())
        {
            Console.WriteLine("Shot has been silenced.");
            return true;
        }

        return false;
    }
}
```

So, we have left the default implementation of Reload method. But our Shoot method had some additional functionality added to it. If the shot has been successful, we notify the console that the shot has been silenced.

Now, we will add another **Decorator**. We will call it ExtendedMagazine. And this is what it will look like:

```
namespace Decorator_Demo;

internal class ExtendedMagazine : GunDecorator
{
    private int extraAmmo = 0;

    public override void Reload()
    {
        base.Reload();
        extraAmmo = 6;
    }

```

```
13      public override bool Shoot()
14      {
15          if (!base.Shoot())
16          {
17              if (extraAmmo > 0)
18              {
19                  Console.WriteLine("Shot fired from the ex\
20  tended magazine.");
21                  extraAmmo--;
22                  return true;
23              }
24
25              return false;
26          }
27
28          return true;
29      }
30  }
```

This **Decorator** provides some additional functionality. Its `Reload` method allows us to apply additional ammo capacity. And its `Shoot` method ensures that if the **Original Object** runs out of ammo, we can still fire shots from the additional ammo reserve.

Now, let's see how these two decorators work together. To do so, we will replace the content of `Program.cs` file with the following:

```
1   using Decorator_Demo;
2
3   var gun = new Gun();
4
5   gun.Reload();
6   gun.Shoot();
7   gun.Shoot();
8
9   Console.WriteLine("Applying a silencer.");
10  var silencer = new Silencer();
11  silencer.SetGun(gun);
12  silencer.Shoot();
13  silencer.Shoot();
14
15  Console.WriteLine("Applying an extended magazine.");
16  var extendedMag = new ExtendedMagazine();
17  extendedMag.SetGun(silencer);
18  extendedMag.Reload();
19  extendedMag.Shoot();
20  extendedMag.Shoot();
21  extendedMag.Shoot();
22  extendedMag.Shoot();
23  extendedMag.Shoot();
24  extendedMag.Shoot();
25  extendedMag.Shoot();
26  extendedMag.Shoot();
27
28  Console.ReadKey();
```

In here, we are creating an instance of the Gun class, reloading it and making some shots. Then we are applying an instance of Silencer to it and shooting via the silencer. Afterwards, we are applying an instance of ExtendedMagazine to it, reloading it and making some shots via it. And you can see the output on the following screenshots:

```
Shot fired.
Shot fired.
Applying a silencer.
Shot fired.
Shot has been silenced.
Shot fired.
Shot has been silenced.
Applying an extended magazine.
Shot fired.
Shot has been silenced.
Shot fired.
Shot has been silenced.
Shot fired.
Shot has been silenced.
Shot fired.
Shot has been silenced.
Shot fired.
Shot has been silenced.
Shot fired.
Shot has been silenced.
Out of ammo.
Shot fired from the extended magazine.
Out of ammo.
Shot fired from the extended magazine.
```

Figure 32.2 - The results of applying multiple decorators

And this concludes our Decorator example. Let's now summarize the main benefits of using this design pattern.

Benefits of using Decorator

The benefits of using Decorator are as follows:

- This design pattern allows you to modify the behavior of objects without having access to internal functionality of those objects.
- It strongly enforces the open-closed principle, so nothing that uses the original objects will have to be modified.
- It enforces single responsibility principle, as each **Decorator** implementation is responsible for a specific functionality.

- It's easy to write automated tests against **Decorator** implementations because they are very specific and focused.

But, despite all of its benefits, Decorator has some caveats. And this is what we will have a look at next.

Caveats of using Composite

It's a good thing that Decorator allows you to apply multiple layers of modified functionality to your **Original Object**. But when you have too many of them in the stack, it may become hard to manage the functionality. Removal and replacement of **Decorator** instances becomes especially problematic. So you need to watch out for that.

In the above example, I have intentionally demonstrated another problem you may encounter while using Decorator. We have added a silencer to our gun, which added silencing functionality to our shots. So far so good. Then we added an extended magazine on top of the silencer. And this combination worked too. That was until we ran out of ammo from the original gun. We could still make shots from the additional ammo reserve, but those were not silenced, making our silencer ineffective in this scenario.

So that exposes a problem. **Decorator** implementations need to be designed in such a way that they don't interfere with each other's functionality.

Finally, there's not always a possibility to use the Decorator pattern when you want to modify the behavior of the objects you can't modify from the inside. Or, at least, you can't modify it in a specific way. And this is where Adapter will be more appropriate.

33. Facade

Facade design pattern is all about building a simple interface to abstract away the complexity of using multiple complex interfaces. If, for example, your application needs to access multiple services and then perform some complex logic of coordinating the responses from those services, Facade design pattern would allow you to isolate such functionality in one place. This will then be accessible by the rest of the application via a simple interface.

A real-life analogy could be a food delivery system. All you do is go to a website and select the items to order. And then those items will get delivered to you. As a consumer, this is all you care about. But behind the scenes, once you place an order, you trigger a whole complex system. The food needs to be prepared. The preparation of different items needs to be coordinated. The driver needs to be assigned. The delivery route needs to be planned. And so on.

Facade can be summarized as follows:

- There are several **Endpoint Interfaces**.
- Either the calls to the **Endpoint Interfaces** need to be coordinated or the responses from them need to be aggregated in some way.
- There is a **Facade** object that performs all of such coordination.
- The **Facade** object is accessible by the rest of the application via a simple interface.

```
                    ┌─────────────────────────┐
                    │        Facade           │
                    ├─────────────────────────┤
                    │  DeliverCombunedData()  │
                    └─────────────────────────┘
```

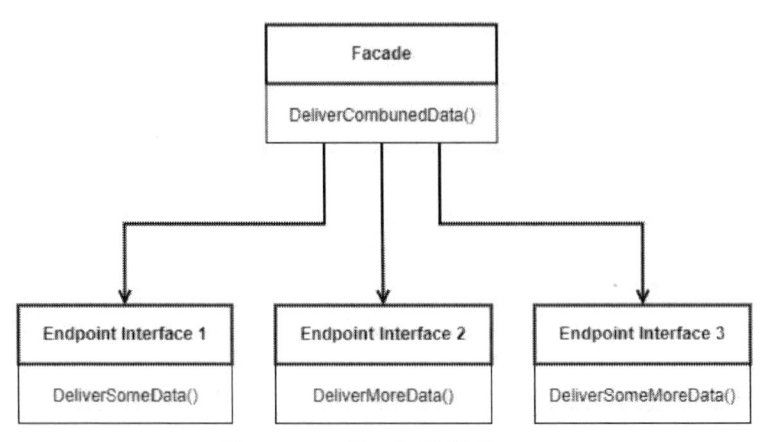

Figure 33.1 - Facade UML diagram

We will now go through an example implementation of Facade. The complete solution can be found via the link below:

https://github.com/fiodarsazanavets/design-patterns-in-csharp/tree/main/Structural_Patterns/Facade

Prerequisites

In order to be able to implement the code samples below, you need the following installed on your machine:

- .NET 6 SDK (or newer)
- A suitable IDE or a code editor (Visual Studio, Visual Studio Code, JetBrains Rider)

Facade implementation example

Imagine that we need to build an application where, if we input the account name, we would be able to retrieve the list of products this account is allowed to buy. But to achieve this, we will have to deal with multiple back-end systems. List of products will be returned based on which category the account belongs to, whether or not the account is a buyer or a reseller. But our application doesn't hold this information. There is another service that will return the account category based on the account id. But our application doesn't store the account id either. It operates within its own bounded context where account id doesn't exist. Only the name of the account is known. So we need to call another service to obtain the account id based on the account name.

As you can see, it's a fairly complex interaction between multiple services. And this is where the Facade design pattern would fit perfectly.

We will start by creating a .NET console application. Then we will add a service that will return a list of accounts. This service would be represented by AccountDataService class and it's definition would be as follows:

```
namespace Facade_Demo;

internal class AccountDataService
{
    private readonly List<Account> accounts;

    public AccountDataService()
    {
        accounts = new();
        accounts.Add(new Account(1, "John Smith"));
        accounts.Add(new Account(2, "Jane Doe"));
        accounts.Add(new Account(3, "Laurence Newport"));
        accounts.Add(new Account(4, "David Fisher"));
    }

    public List<Account> GetAccounts()
```

```
17      {
18          return accounts;
19      }
20  }
21
22  internal record Account
23  {
24      public Account(int id, string name)
25      {
26          Id = id;
27          Name = name;
28      }
29
30      public int Id { get; }
31      public string Name { get; }
32  }
```

So, in here, we are returning a list of Account objects that contain Id and Name properties. For demonstration purposes, we are hard-coding the data. But in a real-life scenario, the data would be retrieved from a data storage of some sort.

Next, we will add a service that will allow us to retrieve the account category based on the account id. The service will be called AccountCategoryService and it will look as follows:

```
1   namespace Facade_Demo;
2
3   internal class AccountCategoryService
4   {
5       private Dictionary<int, AccountCategory> accountCateg\
6   ories;
7
8       public AccountCategoryService()
9       {
10          accountCategories = new();
```

```
11                accountCategories.Add(1, AccountCategory.Buyer);
12                accountCategories.Add(2, AccountCategory.Buyer);
13                accountCategories.Add(3, AccountCategory.Reseller\
14    );
15                accountCategories.Add(4, AccountCategory.Reseller\
16    );
17        }
18
19        public AccountCategory GetCategory(int accountId)
20        {
21            return accountCategories[accountId];
22        }
23    }
24
25    internal enum AccountCategory
26    {
27        Buyer = 1,
28        Reseller = 2
29    }
```

After this, we will add a service that will give us a list of products based on the account category. We will call it ProductsDataService and we will define it as this:

```
1    namespace Facade_Demo;
2
3    internal class ProductsDataService
4    {
5        private readonly Dictionary<int, List<Product>> produ\
6    ctLists;
7
8        public ProductsDataService()
9        {
10            productLists = new();
11            productLists[1] = new List<Product>
```

```
            {
                new Product("Product 1", 9.99),
                new Product("Product 2", 19.99)
            };

            productLists[2] = new List<Product>
            {
                new Product("Bundle 1", 99.99),
                new Product("Bundle 2", 199.99)
            };
        }

        public List<Product> GetProductsForCategory(int categ\
oryId)
        {
            return productLists[categoryId];
        }
    }

    internal record Product
    {
        public Product(string name, double price)
        {
            Name = name;
            Price = price;
        }

        public string Name { get; }
        public double Price { get; }
    }
```

Finally, we are ready to add our **Facade** object. We will call this class ProductsFacade. And its definition would be as follows:

```csharp
namespace Facade_Demo;

internal class ProductsFacade
{
    private readonly AccountCategoryService accountCategoryService;
    private readonly AccountDataService accountDataService;
    private readonly ProductsDataService productDataService;

    public ProductsFacade()
    {
        accountCategoryService = new();
        accountDataService = new();
        productDataService = new();
    }

    public List<Product> GetProductListForAccount(string name)
    {
        var accountId = accountDataService
                        .GetAccounts()
                        .Where(a => a.Name == name)
                        .Select(a => a.Id)
                        .FirstOrDefault();

        if (accountId == default)
            return new List<Product>();

        var accountCategory = accountCategoryService.GetCategory(accountId);

        return productDataService.GetProductsForCategory((int)accountCategory);
```

```
36        }
37    }
```

As you can see, we are coordinating the work between the services we have created earlier. We are first retrieving the accounts from an instance of AccountDataService and retrieving the account id from it that is associated with the name that has been inputted. Then, we are retrieving the account category from an instance of AccountCategoryService. Finally, we are converting this category to an integer and we are using it to retrieve the actual product list from an instance of ProductsDataService. This list is then returned to the caller.

Of course, in a real-life application, we would inject interfaces of the **Endpoint Service** objects rather than concrete implementations of them into our **Facade** object. Plus the **Facade** object itself would implement an interface. This would make it consistent with the dependency inversion principle. But to make the demonstration as simple as possible, we are using concrete instances.

Now, we can see how this logic operates. And to do so, we will replace the content of Program.cs file with the following:

```
1   using Facade_Demo;
2
3   var facade = new ProductsFacade();
4
5   foreach (var product in facade.GetProductListForAccount("\
6   John Smith"))
7   {
8       Console.WriteLine($"Product name: {product.Name}");
9       Console.WriteLine($"Product price: {product.Price}");
10  }
11
12  Console.ReadKey();
```

And the output of this program would look like this:

```
Product name: Product 1
Product price: 9.99
Product name: Product 2
Product price: 19.99
```

Figure 33.2 - Output returned by the Facade object

And this concludes the overview of Facade design pattern. Let's summarize its main benefits.

Benefits of using Facade

Facade design pattern has the following as its main benefits:

- It allows you to isolate complex coordinating logic in a single place of the application.
- It allows this complex coordinating logic to be easily reused.
- The Facade object can be easily mocked in automated tests.

And now we will have a look at some of the caveats that you need to be aware of while using Facade.

Caveats of using Facade

Perhaps the only caveat of using Facade is that it can easily become the so-called *God object* that violates the single responsibility principle. Therefore the developers need to be careful to ensure this doesn't happen. Perhaps, it would make sense to split the coordinating logic into multiple classes and get the **Facade** object to work with them.

34. Flyweight

Flyweight design pattern makes it possible to cram large quantities of objects into the memory without using too much memory. This is made possible by sharing some part of the state between the objects.

For example, imagine a real-time strategy game where you can build huge armies. Each unit is a separate object. But units can have certain states that make them behave differently. For example, a shielded unit behaves differently from a unit without a shield. So, instead of giving the full set of possible behaviors to each unit, why not simply create two instances of an object representing the behavior - shielded and unshielded, and then simply link each unit to one of those instances?

Flyweight can be summarized as follows:

- **Flyweight** object represents a set of some properties.
- **Flyweight Factory** allows you to select a specific instance of the **Flyweight** object.
- Objects that are intended to be multiplied can access a specific instance of the **Flyweight** via the **Flyweight Factory**.

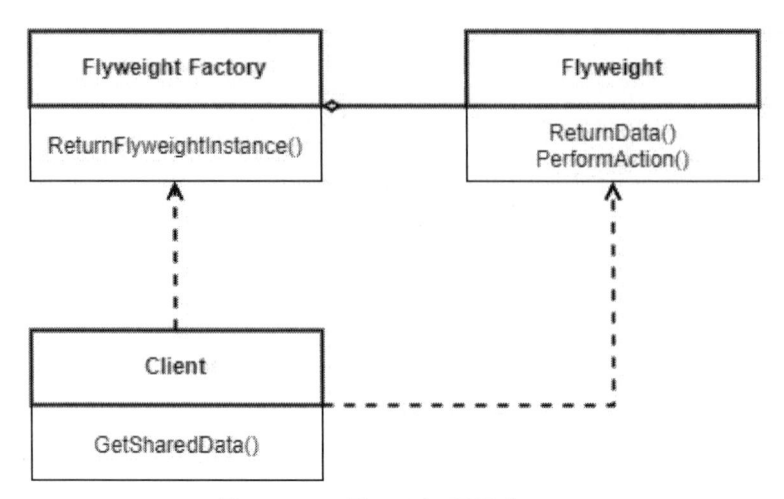

Figure 34.1 - Flyweight UML diagram

We will now go through an example implementation of Flyweight. The complete solution can be found via the link below:

https://github.com/fiodarsazanavets/design-patterns-in-csharp/tree/main/Structural_Patterns/Flyweight

Prerequisites

In order to be able to implement the code samples below, you need the following installed on your machine:

- .NET 6 SDK (or newer)
- A suitable IDE or a code editor (Visual Studio, Visual Studio Code, JetBrains Rider)

Flyweight implementation example

Let's imagine that we are building a strategy video game that would allow the player to build large armies. This army would consist of different types of soldiers. But all these soldier types would have some common properties. Only that the values of these properties would be different for different soldier types.

In our example, we will use the .NET console application project template. And then we will add the SoldierFlyweight class to it that will represent a set of shared characteristics for our soldiers. The definition of this class will be as follows:

```
internal class SoldierFlyweight
{
    public SoldierFlyweight(string soldierType,
        int experienceLevel,
        int speed,
        int strength)
    {
        SoldierType = soldierType;
        ExperienceLevel = experienceLevel;
        Speed = speed;
        Strength = strength;
    }

    public string SoldierType { get; set; }
    public int ExperienceLevel { get; set; }
    public int Speed { get; set; }
    public int Strength { get; set; }

    public void Eliminate(int soldierId)
    {
        Console.WriteLine($"{SoldierType} {soldierId} has\
 been eliminated.");
    }
}
```

The class has a range of properties. And it also comes with the Eliminate method, which triggers some behavior when a specific soldier gets eliminated.

Then, we will add **Flyweight Factory** object that will allow us to select a specific instance of the SoldierFlyweight class. For this, we will have FlyweightFactory class, which will have the following code:

```csharp
namespace Flyweight_Demo;

internal class FlyweightFactory
{
    private Dictionary<string, SoldierFlyweight> flyweights;

    public FlyweightFactory()
    {
        flyweights = new();
        flyweights["Militiaman"] = new SoldierFlyweight("Militiaman", 1, 1, 1);
        flyweights["Soldier"] = new SoldierFlyweight("Soldier", 2, 1, 2);
        flyweights["Knight"] = new SoldierFlyweight("Soldier", 10, 5, 5);
    }

    public SoldierFlyweight GetFlyweight(string key)
    {
        return flyweights[key];
    }
}
```

This allows us to define a number of specific soldier types. Now, we will create an army of soldiers. To do so, we will replace the content of Program.cs file with the following:

```csharp
1   using Flyweight_Demo;
2
3   var factory = new FlyweightFactory();
4   var army = new Dictionary<int, SoldierFlyweight>();
5
6   Console.WriteLine("Adding militiamen to the army.");
7   for (var i = 0; i < 1000; i++)
8   {
9       army[i] = factory.GetFlyweight("Militiaman");
10  }
11
12  Console.WriteLine("Adding soldiers to the army.");
13  for (var i = 0; i < 100; i++)
14  {
15      army[i + 1000] = factory.GetFlyweight("Soldier");
16  }
17
18  Console.WriteLine("Adding knights to the army.");
19  for (var i = 0; i < 10; i++)
20  {
21      army[i + 1100] = factory.GetFlyweight("Knight");
22  }
23
24  Console.WriteLine($"Total army size is {army.Count}.");
25
26  Console.ReadKey();
```

The output of this program would be as follows:

```
Adding militiamen to the army.
Adding soldiers to the army.
Adding knights to the army.
Total army size is 1110.
```

Figure 34.2 - Using flyweight objects to build an army

This code demonstrates obvious benefits of using Flyweight design pattern. Even though we are storing many objects representing soldiers in the memory, we are only reserving a small amount of memory for each soldier. This is because each of the items representing a soldier refers to one of only three instances of a **Flyweight** object that represents a bulk of its functionality. And because we have a parametrized `Eliminate` method on our **Flyweight** object, we can still perform some behavior that is specific to an individual soldier.

Benefits of using Flyweight

So, the core benefits of using Flyweight design pattern are as follows:

- It allows you to use memory very efficiently by sharing large chunks of the state between objects.
- It allows you to still perform functionality that is specific to a particular item instance.

But to use Flyweight effectively, one needs to be aware of its caveats. And this is what we will have a look at next.

Caveats of using Flyweight

Perhaps the main caveat of using Flyweight is that it can make the code complicated and difficult to read. Therefore sometimes there needs to be a trade-off between code maintainability and the efficient use of RAM.

Another disadvantage of using flyweight is that, although it will save your memory, it might actually increase the CPU usage. Imagine many objects making a parametrized call to a specific instance of a **Flyweight** object. Even if this instance is shared between many objects, your CPU would still be doing a lot of work in this situation.

35. Proxy

Proxy design pattern allows you to cache the results of computationally expensive operations. With this design pattern, you don't have to run such an operation every single time you need the results. On subsequent requests, the results are simply retrieved from the cache.

It's analogous to how the cache in a browser works. When you visit a web page for the first time, the browser will retrieve it from the server. But it will then store a copy of this page in its own cache. So when you visit the page next time, it will be retrieved from the local cache. In this situation, the browser is acting as a proxy for the server.

Proxy can be summarized as follows:

- There is a **Main Service** object that is computationally expensive to run.
- There is a **Proxy** object that implements exactly the same interface as the **Main Service**.
- All requests to the **Main Service** are performed via the **Proxy**
- **Proxy** only runs the expensive operation on the **Main Service** when it needs to and then it caches the results.
- Under any other circumstances, **Proxy** returns the results from its cache without contacting the **Main Service**.

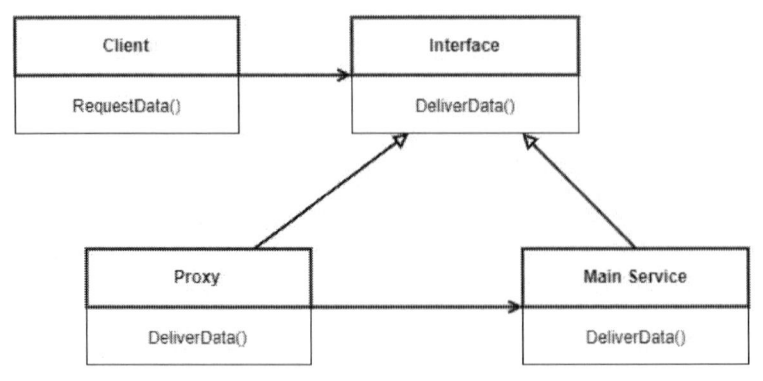

Figure 35.1 - Proxy UML diagram

We will now go through an example implementation of Proxy. The complete solution can be found via the link below:

https://github.com/fiodarsazanavets/design-patterns-in-csharp/tree/main/Structural_Patterns/Proxy

Prerequisites

In order to be able to implement the code samples below, you need the following installed on your machine:

- .NET 6 SDK (or newer)
- A suitable IDE or a code editor (Visual Studio, Visual Studio Code, JetBrains Rider)

Proxy implementation example

Let's imagine that we have some back-end service that we can retrieve data from and submit new data to. But retrieving the data happens to be a long and computationally expensive process. And this is what we will simulate to demonstrate how the Proxy design pattern can be applied to solve such a problem.

We will create a new .NET console application and we will add IDataService interface to it, which will look as follows:

```
1  namespace Proxy_Demo;
2
3  internal interface IDataService
4  {
5      Task<List<string>> GetData();
6      void InsertData(string item);
7  }
```

Then we will add an implementation of this interface that represents our **Main Service**. It will be represented by DataService class with the following content:

```
1  namespace Proxy_Demo;
2
3  internal class DataService : IDataService
4  {
5      private readonly List<string> data;
6
7      public DataService()
8      {
9          data = new();
10     }
11
12     public async Task<List<string>> GetData()
13     {
14         // Simulate long-running process
15         await Task.Delay(3000);
16         return data;
17     }
18
```

```
19      public void InsertData(string item)
20      {
21          data.Add(item);
22      }
23  }
```

So, we are simulating a long-running data retrieval process by adding a three second delay to the GetData method.

Next, we will add a **Proxy** implementation of the same interface. The class will be called DataServiceProxy and it will look as follows:

```
1   namespace Proxy_Demo;
2
3   internal class DataServiceProxy : IDataService
4   {
5       private readonly DataService dataService;
6       private List<string>? localCache;
7
8       public DataServiceProxy()
9       {
10          dataService = new DataService();
11          localCache = null;
12      }
13
14      public async Task<List<string>> GetData()
15      {
16          Console.WriteLine($"{DateTime.Now} - Started data\
17  query.");
18
19          if (localCache is null)
20              localCache = await dataService.GetData();
21
22          Console.WriteLine($"{DateTime.Now} - Data has bee\
23  n retrieved.");
24          return localCache;
```

```
25        }
26
27        public void InsertData(string item)
28        {
29            localCache = null;
30            dataService.InsertData(item);
31        }
32  }
```

This proxy acts as a middleware between the actual service implementation and the caller. It maintains its own cache, which is instantiated as `null` and gets reset to `null` every time new data is inserted via the **Main Service**. But once it has retrieved the **Main Service**, the proxy populates its own cache with it. And while the cache has any items in it, any subsequent call to `GetData` method will use the cache and won't call the **Main Service**.

To make the benefits of using Proxy design pattern obvious, we can replace the content of the `Program.cs` file with the following:

```
1   using Proxy_Demo;
2
3   var dataService = new DataServiceProxy();
4   dataService.InsertData("item 1");
5   dataService.InsertData("item 2");
6   dataService.InsertData("item 3");
7
8   var data = await dataService.GetData();
9   Console.WriteLine($"Items retrieved: {data.Count}");
10  data = await dataService.GetData();
11  Console.WriteLine($"Items retrieved: {data.Count}");
12
13  Console.ReadKey();
```

In here, where are initially inserting three items via the **Proxy**. Then, we retrieve this data twice, comparing the time it took for the data to be retrieved.

As the following screenshot demonstrates, the data took three seconds to arrive on the first run. But its retrieval was almost instant on the second run. And this is because, on the first run, the **Proxy** ran an expensive operation on the **Main Service**, while on the second run it used its own cache.

```
22/02/2022 08:56:48 - Started data query.
22/02/2022 08:56:51 - Data has been retrieved.
Items retrieved: 3
22/02/2022 08:56:51 - Started data query.
22/02/2022 08:56:51 - Data has been retrieved.
Items retrieved: 3
```

Figure 35.2 - **Performance improvements by using Proxy**

And this concludes the overview of Proxy design pattern. Let's summarize its main benefits.

Benefits of using Proxy

The benefits of using Proxy can be summarized as follows:

- This design pattern allows you not to run expensive operations every time you need to obtain the results of these operations.
- Because the **Proxy** object uses the same interface as the **Main Service**, **Proxy** object can be used in any place in the code where the **Main Service** is normally used.

But, as with any design patterns, there are still some caveats to be aware of while making a decision on whether or not to use Proxy.

Caveats of using Proxy

While using Proxy, you have to strike a good balance between performance and accuracy. You need to put some logic in place to make sure that your cache is not refreshed too often. But at the same time, you need to ensure the cache is reasonably accurate. If the cache refreshes too often, you may lose the benefits of using Proxy. If it doesn't refresh often enough, it may become outdated quickly. So, when making design decisions, you need to consider this trade-off.

Other than that, using the Proxy design pattern will make your code more complicated. And if you are dealing with complex logic, this may make your code harder to read and maintain. So the tradeoff between the performance and readability might be another point to consider while using Proxy.

Behavioral design patterns

Behavioral design patterns tell us how objects are supposed to behave. This section covers the following patterns:

- Chain of Responsibility
- Command
- Iterator
- Mediator
- Memento
- Observer
- State
- Strategy
- Template Method
- Visitor

36. Chain of Responsibility

Chain of Responsibility is a design pattern that allows you to apply multiple processing steps to an action. Any step of the process may have a condition added to it, which will allow it to exit the process immediately and not execute any further steps.

Perhaps, the best-known example of Chain of Responsibility design pattern in .NET is ASP.NET Core middleware[2]. This is where you can apply multiple stages of processing to incoming HTTP requests. The request will not get to its destination until it goes through all the steps, which you, as an application developer, can add or remove at will. For example, you can add a step that will verify whether or not the user is authorized. Then, if so, the request will proceed to the next stage of processing. If not, the response will be returned immediately with an appropriate response code.

Chain of Responsibility can be summarized as follows:

- There is either an abstract class or an interface that represent a **Handler** object.
- The **Handler** has a method to set its **Successor**, which would be another instance of the **Handler** object.
- The **Handler** would also have the definition of the actual method that would represent the processing step.
- Each concrete implementation of a **Handler** would have some logic inside this method, which, after performing its own processing, would call the same method on the **Successor** (if one is set).

[2]https://docs.microsoft.com/en-us/aspnet/core/fundamentals/middleware/

- The method may also have a condition which will allow it to short-circuit the process and return immediately.

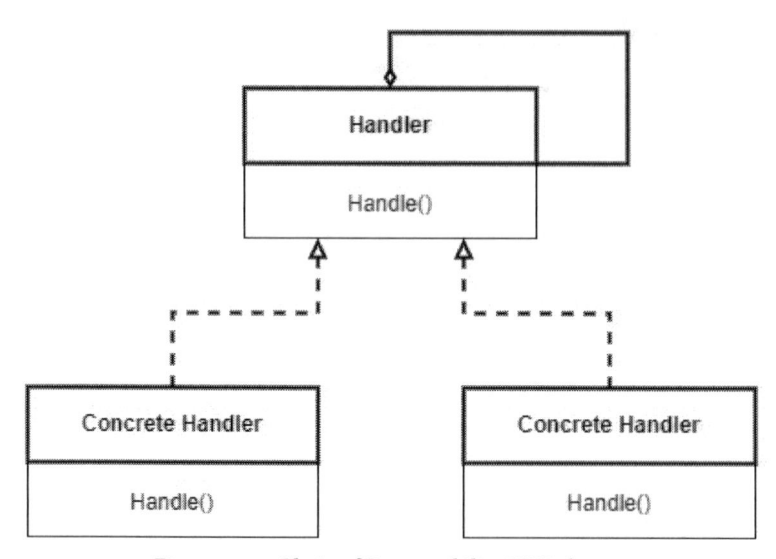

Figure 36.1 - Chain of Responsibility UML diagram

We will now go through an example implementation of Chain of Responsibility. The complete solution can be found via the link below:

https://github.com/fiodarsazanavets/design-patterns-in-csharp/tree/main/Behavioral_Patterns/Chain-of-Responsibility

Prerequisites

In order to be able to implement the code samples below, you need the following installed on your machine:

- .NET 6 SDK (or newer)
- A suitable IDE or a code editor (Visual Studio, Visual Studio Code, JetBrains Rider)

Chain of Responsibility implementation example

To demonstrate Chain of Responsibility, we will use a simplified request processing example, similar to what ASP.NET Core middleware uses. But, as this is just a conceptual representation of request processing and not an actual thing, we won't have to build a fully-fledged web application. We will create a simple console app.

Once created, we will add classes to it that will represent our Request and Response objects. Our Request object will look like this:

```
namespace Chain_of_Responsibility_Demo;

internal class Request
{
    public string? Username { get; set; }
    public string? Password { get; set; }
    public string? Role { get; set; }
}
```

And here is what our Response object will look like:

```
namespace Chain_of_Responsibility_Demo;

internal class Response
{
    public Response(bool success, string message)
    {
        Success = success;
        Message = message;
    }

    public bool Success { get; }
```

```
        public string? Message { get; }
}
```

Next, we will add a representation of a **Handler**. In our case, it will be RequestHandler.cs file with the following content:

```
namespace Chain_of_Responsibility_Demo;

internal abstract class RequestHandler
{
    protected RequestHandler? successor;

    public abstract Response HandleRequest(Request reques\
t);

    public void SetNext(RequestHandler successor)
    {
        this.successor = successor;
    }
}
```

In here, we have a protected successor field, which represents the next instance of a **Handler** in the chain. Because the process of setting the successor will be identical for any concrete **Handler**, we have a non-virtual SetNext method. And the main processing step is represented by HandleRequest method, which is abstract, because it will be specific to each specific **Handler** implementation.

And now we will start adding specific implementations of it. First, we will add AuthenticationHandler.cs file with the following content:

```csharp
namespace Chain_of_Responsibility_Demo;

internal class AuthenticationHandler : RequestHandler
{
    public override Response HandleRequest(Request reques\
t)
    {
        if (request.Username != "John" ||
            request.Password != "password")
            return new Response(false, "Invalid username \
or password.");

        if (successor is not null)
            return successor.HandleRequest(request);

        return new Response(true, "Authentication success\
ful.");
    }
}
```

In here, purely for demo purposes, we are checking whether the request contains a specific username and password. Of course, in a real-life scenario, you wouldn't use hardcoded values. But we are using them here for the sake of simplicity.

If either the username or the password doesn't match, we return the call immediately. Otherwise, we either call the HandleRequest method on the **Successor**, if one is set, or just return a response that indicates success.

Next, we will add a AuthorizationHandler.cs file with the following content:

```csharp
namespace Chain_of_Responsibility_Demo;

internal class AuthorizationHandler : RequestHandler
{
    public override Response HandleRequest(Request request)
    {
        if (request.Role != "Admin")
            return new Response(false, "User not authorized.");

        if (successor is not null)
            return successor.HandleRequest(request);

        return new Response(true, "Authorization successful.");
    }
}
```

This is an authorization handler. The idea behind it is that, even if a correct username and password were provided, the user may still not be authorized to access the resource. In this case, we are only allowing access to a user that has a role of Admin. Otherwise, the process is the same as before. Call the successor if one is set. Return a response with a success code otherwise.

Now, to bring it all together, we will replace the content of Program.cs file with the following:

```csharp
using Chain_of_Responsibility_Demo;

var handler1 = new AuthenticationHandler();
var handler2 = new AuthorizationHandler();
handler1.SetNext(handler2);

var request1 = new Request
{
    Username = "Invalid",
    Password = "Invalid",
};

var request2 = new Request
{
    Username = "John",
    Password = "password",
    Role = "User"
};

var request3 = new Request
{
    Username = "John",
    Password = "password",
    Role = "Admin"
};

var response1 = handler1.HandleRequest(request1);
var response2 = handler1.HandleRequest(request2);
var response3 = handler1.HandleRequest(request3);
Console.WriteLine($"Response 1: Success - {response1.Succ\
ess}, Message - {response1.Message}");
Console.WriteLine($"Response 2: Success - {response2.Succ\
ess}, Message - {response2.Message}");
Console.WriteLine($"Response 3: Success - {response3.Succ\
ess}, Message - {response3.Message}");
```

```
36
37    Console.ReadKey();
```

So, we are setting our Chain of Responsibility up in such a way that `AuthorizationHandler` is the successor of `AuthenticationHandler`. Then, we send three requests to it to see what responses we would get. In the first request, we have provided the wrong username and password. In the second request, the username and password are correct, but the role is wrong from the perspective of `AuthorizationHandler`. In the third request, the username, the password, and the role are correct.

And this is the result that we get:

```
Response 1: Success - False, Message - Invalid username or password.
Response 2: Success - False, Message - User not authorized.
Response 3: Success - True, Message - Authorization successful.
```

Figure 36.2 - Chain of Responsibility in action

As we expected, the first message indicates that `AuthenticationHandler` has marked the response as a failure. The second message indicates that `AuthorizationHandler` has marked the response as a failure. The third message indicates that `AuthorizationHandler` has marked the response as a success.

And this concludes the overview of Chain of Responsibility design pattern. Let's summarize its main benefits.

Benefits of using Chain of Responsibility

The benefits of using Chain of Responsibility can be summarized as follows:

- Processing stages can be easily added and removed at will.

- Single responsibility principle is well implemented, as each processing step is isolated in its own implementation.
- Open-closed principle is well implemented, as you can add new functionality without modifying any existing classes.

Of course, Chain of Responsibility has its own caveats. And this is what we will have a look at next.

Caveats of using Chain of Responsibility

There aren't really many caveats of using Chain of Responsibility. But what you really need to watch out for is that you may end up with your requests remaining unhandled if you make your chain too complex and misplace any of its links.

It's not always possible to make each concrete **Handler** implementation agnostic of the step its used in. For example, checking whether a user is authorized to access a resource would be meaningless if we haven't already checked whether or not the user is authenticated. And this is exactly the reason why accidentally misplacing the steps may cause your chain to fail.

So, when using this design pattern, you need to always think about such a scenario. If it's possible, make each **Handler** implementation agnostic of the sequence of the steps it's used in. If it can't be done - make sure that sufficient documentation is provided.

37. Command

Command is a design pattern that isolates an operation in its own object. This makes such an operation reusable, so you don't have to construct a brand new logic every time you need to perform such an operation.

The most popular way of using Command is in database operations. A Command object will contain all necessary information to perform some action that would modify the data (insertion, update, deletion, etc.). Then, if you need to perform such an operation on a particular database table, all you have to do is just reuse this object and maybe modify some of its parameters. You won't have to write any complex logic involving object-relationship mappers or direct database queries.

Command can be summarized as follows:

- There is a **Command** interface that describes the behavior that each command should have. Usually, it only has one method, which executes the action.
- If multiple related commands are needed, it makes sense to add **Command** abstract class with the shared functionality.
- Each **Concrete Command** accepts parameters in its constructor and implements the method that executes the action.
- Because **Command** accepts constructor parameters, it's intended to be a single-use object.
- Optionally, there could be an **Invoker** object, the role of which is to decide which commands to execute.

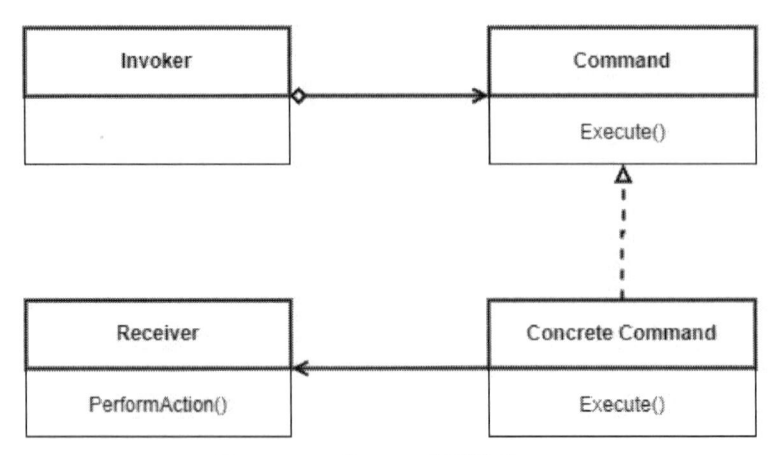

Figure 37.1 - **Command UML diagram**

We will now go through an example implementation of Command. The complete solution can be found via the link below:

https://github.com/fiodarsazanavets/design-patterns-in-csharp/tree/main/Behavioral_Patterns/Command

Prerequisites

In order to be able to implement the code samples below, you need the following installed on your machine:

- .NET 6 SDK (or newer)
- A suitable IDE or a code editor (Visual Studio, Visual Studio Code, JetBrains Rider)

Command implementation example

As in all other examples, we will create a console application project. And the first thing we will do in this project is add the interface for our **Command** object, which will be as follows:

```
1   namespace Command_Demo;
2
3   internal interface ICommand
4   {
5       void Execute();
6   }
```

As you can see, the only method we have is Execute. In our example, it's blocking void. But it could be an asynchronous Task where appropriate. **Command** is meant to execute something rather than return data. This is why there is no return value in our example.

Next, we will add DataReceiver.cs file with the following content:

```
1   namespace Command_Demo;
2
3   internal class DataReceiver
4   {
5       private readonly Dictionary<string, string> data;
6
7       public DataReceiver()
8       {
9           data = new Dictionary<string, string>();
10      }
11
12      public void Upsert(string key, string value)
13      {
14          data[key] = value;
15          Console.WriteLine($"Upserted: {key} - {value}.");
16      }
17
18      public void Delete(string key)
19      {
20          if (data.ContainsKey(key))
21          {
22              data.Remove(key);
```

```
23              Console.WriteLine($"Removed: {key}.");
24          }
25      }
26  }
```

This file mimics a database access layer. You can imagine that, instead of dealing with in-memory Dictionary, you are working with a database table.

Next, we will add the following abstract class. We will need this, because all of our commands will depend on DataReceiver we've created earlier. So we put it into the constructor.

```
1   namespace Command_Demo;
2
3   internal abstract class Command : ICommand
4   {
5       protected DataReceiver receiver;
6
7       public Command(DataReceiver receiver)
8       {
9           this.receiver = receiver;
10      }
11
12      public abstract void Execute();
13  }
```

Next, we will add the following **Concrete Command** instance, which performs upsertion (insertion or update) of values into the DataReceiver.

```csharp
namespace Command_Demo;

internal class UpsertCommand : Command
{
    private string key;
    private string value;

    public UpsertCommand(string key,
        string value,
        DataReceiver receiver) : base(receiver)
    {
        this.key = key;
        this.value = value;
    }

    public override void Execute()
    {
        receiver.Upsert(key, value);
    }
}
```

Then, we will add the following **Concrete Command**, which deletes a specified entry from the DataReceiver based on its key.

```csharp
namespace Command_Demo;

internal class DeleteCommand : Command
{
    private string key;

    public DeleteCommand(string key,
        DataReceiver receiver) : base(receiver)
    {
        this.key = key;
    }
```

```
12
13      public override void Execute()
14      {
15          receiver.Delete(key);
16      }
17  }
```

In our example, we will also add a command **Invoker**. It's not strictly necessary, as you can use **Command** instance directly by the calling code. But it's still useful for demonstration purposes.

```
1   namespace Command_Demo;
2
3   internal class DataCommandInvoker
4   {
5       private ICommand? command;
6
7       public void SetCommand(ICommand command)
8       {
9           this.command = command;
10          Console.WriteLine($"Command {command.GetType()} s\
11  et.");
12      }
13
14      public void ExecuteCommand()
15      {
16          command?.Execute();
17      }
18  }
```

Finally, we will replace the content of Program.cs file with the following:

```
1  using Command_Demo;
2
3  var dataReceiver = new DataReceiver();
4  var invoker = new DataCommandInvoker();
5  invoker.SetCommand(new UpsertCommand("item1", "value1", d\
6  ataReceiver));
7  invoker.ExecuteCommand();
8  invoker.SetCommand(new DeleteCommand("item1", dataReceive\
9  r));
10 invoker.ExecuteCommand();
11 Console.ReadKey();
```

Essentially, what we are doing here. is inserting an item into our data collection and then deleting this item from it. And this is what the output shows:

```
Command Command_Demo.UpsertCommand set.
Upserted: item1 - value1.
Command Command_Demo.DeleteCommand set.
Removed: item1.
```

Figure 37.2 - **Commands successfully executed**

And this concludes the overview of Command design pattern. Let's summarize its main benefits.

Benefits of using Command

Command design pattern has the following benefits:

- Single responsibility principle is well maintained, as the operation is fully separated from the objects it operates on.
- Open-closed principle is well maintained, as the operation is added in a separate class without modifying any existing classes.

- You can easily reuse a **Command** implementation if you want to perform a number of similar operations.
- You can combine it with Chain of Responsibility and assemble multiple simple commands into one complex command.
- You can combine it with Memento and enable undo/redo actions.
- Because the entire process of execution is controlled within a **Command** implementation, you can fully control the execution logic, including any delays to it.

Let's now have a look at things to look out for while using the Command design pattern.

Caveats of using Command

Perhaps the main thing you have to look out for while using Command is that you can accidentally make your code too complicated if you are not careful enough.

First of all, you may end up with too many **Command** objects that will become hard to manage. However, it might be that not every operation that you need to perform warrants the use of Command. For example, if an operation is definitely neither customizable nor reusable, it may not be needed to be isolated into its own **Command** object.

Secondly, if you make any particular **Command** implementation too customizable, you may end up with a badly written object that is trying to do too many things at once and violates single responsibility principle as the result. So, it's OK to have some customization in a **Command** implementation. But make sure it's only some relatively minor customization.

Remember that Command, just like any other design patterns, is meant to make your code more maintainable and not less maintainable.

38. Iterator

Iterator is a design pattern that allows a developer to encapsulate a collection of any complexity inside an object with a very simple interface. The consumers of this interface would be able to iterate through each individual item of this collection without knowing any of its implementation details.

In C#, pretty much any inbuilt collection data types that can be traversed inside a `for each` loop are based on the Iterator design pattern. For example, they expose methods such as `MoveNext`, which are commonly used by this design pattern.

Iterator design pattern can be summarized as follows:

- There is an object known either as an **Aggregate** or a **Collection**. This object stores the actual collection of objects. And this collection can be of any structure and any complexity (trees, stacks, arrays, etc.).
- There is an object called **Iterator**, the role of which is to read the items from the **Aggregate** and expose them to the outside world one by one.
- **Iterator** object reads items in a specific order and keeps track of the current item.

38. Iterator

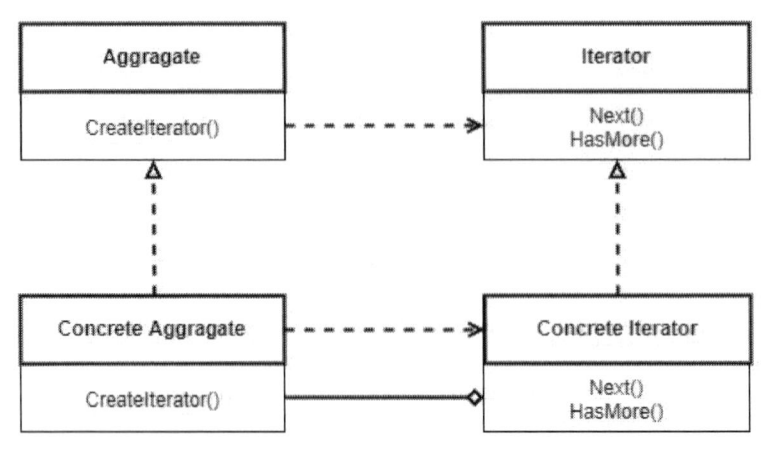

```
┌─────────────────────────┐              ┌─────────────────────────┐
│       Aggragate         │              │        Iterator         │
├─────────────────────────┤              ├─────────────────────────┤
│    CreateIterator()     │- - - - - - ->│         Next()          │
│                         │              │        HasMore()        │
└─────────────────────────┘              └─────────────────────────┘
             △                                       △
             ┊                                       ┊
             ┊                                       ┊
             ┊                                       ┊
┌─────────────────────────┐              ┌─────────────────────────┐
│    Concrete Aggragate   │- - - - - - ->│    Concrete Iterator    │
├─────────────────────────┤              ├─────────────────────────┤
│    CreateIterator()     │─────────────◇│         Next()          │
│                         │              │        HasMore()        │
└─────────────────────────┘              └─────────────────────────┘
```

Figure 38.1 - Iterator UML diagram

We will now go through an example implementation of Iterator. The complete solution can be found via the link below:

https://github.com/fiodarsazanavets/design-patterns-in-csharp/tree/main/Behavioral_Patterns/Iterator

Prerequisites

In order to be able to implement the code samples below, you need the following installed on your machine:

- .NET 6 SDK (or newer)
- A suitable IDE or a code editor (Visual Studio, Visual Studio Code, JetBrains Rider)

Iterator implementation example

We will create a console application project. And the first thing that we will add to this project would be the following interface:

```
1  namespace Iterator_Demo;
2
3  internal interface IIterator
4  {
5      bool MoveNext();
6      int GetCurrent();
7  }
```

This is our **Iterator** interface. It has two methods: MoveNext and GetCurrent. MoveNext method would iterate through each item of the collection and update the pointer to the current item. It will return true if it is possible to move to the next item and it will return false if there are no more items left.

GetCurrent will retrieve the current value from the collection. For the sake of simplicity, we are dealing with the collections of int in our example. However, in a real-life application, you may want your **Itrator** to be generic and get it to work with collections of any data type.

Next, we will create an interface for our **Aggregate**, which will be as follows:

```
1  namespace Iterator_Demo;
2
3  internal interface IAggregate
4  {
5      IIterator CreateIterator();
6      void Insert(int value);
7  }
```

In our case, this interface allows us to retrieve the **Iterator** and insert an item into the collection.

Next, we will add a concrete **Aggregate** that implements this interface. We will start with a basic **Aggregate** that simply encapsulates a List of values.

```
1   namespace Iterator_Demo;
2
3   internal class ListAggregate : IAggregate
4   {
5       private List<int> collection;
6
7       public ListAggregate()
8       {
9           collection = new List<int>();
10      }
11
12      public IIterator CreateIterator()
13      {
14          return new ListIterator(this);
15      }
16
17      public int Count
18      {
19          get { return collection.Count; }
20      }
21
22      public int this[int index]
23      {
24          get { return collection[index]; }
25          set { collection.Insert(index, value); }
26      }
27
28      public void Insert(int value)
29      {
30          collection.Add(value);
31      }
32  }
```

Then, we will add an **Iterator** for this **Aggregate** type. All we do inside this iterator is go through each item of the collection, which maintains the index of the current item. If there are no more items left,MoveNext method will return false.

```csharp
namespace Iterator_Demo;

internal class ListIterator : IIterator
{
    private ListAggregate aggregate;
    private int currentIndex;

    public ListIterator(ListAggregate aggregate)
    {
        this.aggregate = aggregate;
        currentIndex = -1;
    }

    public bool MoveNext()
    {
        if (currentIndex + 1 < aggregate.Count)
        {
            currentIndex++;
            return true;
        }

        return false;
    }

    public int GetCurrent()
    {
        return aggregate[currentIndex];
    }
}
```

But now, we will add something more interesting. What if we had an **Aggregate** that stores data on a sorted binary tree? This would be more complicated than dealing with a flat List. And this is where the Iterator design pattern truly shows its usefulness.

Before we add the new **Aggregate**, we will need to add an object that will represent a node on such a tree. And this is what it will look like:

```
namespace Iterator_Demo;

internal class Node
{
    public Node(int value)
    {
        Value = value;
    }

    public int Value { get; set; }
    public Node Left { get; set; }
    public Node Right { get; set; }
    public Node Parent { get; set; }
}
```

We can now start adding our **Aggregate** that will deal with such a data type. We have called our class SortedBinaryTreeCollection to demonstrate that **Aggregate** and **Collection** are interchangeable names in the context of Iterator design pattern.

```
namespace Iterator_Demo;

internal class SortedBinaryTreeCollection : IAggregate
{
    private Node? root;

    public SortedBinaryTreeCollection()
    {
        root = null;
    }
```

```
12      public IIterator CreateIterator()
13      {
14          return new SortedBinaryTreeIterator(this);
15      }
16
17      public Node GetFirst()
18      {
19          var current = root;
20
21          while (true)
22          {
23              if (current?.Left is not null)
24              {
25                  current = current.Left;
26              }
27              else
28              {
29                  return current;
30              }
31          }
32      }
33  }
```

Then, we will add the following method, which will allow us to insert new values into the tree, while maintaining all the values in the right order:

```
 1  public void Insert(int value)
 2  {
 3      Node newNode = new Node(value);
 4
 5      if (root is null)
 6      {
 7          root = newNode;
 8      }
 9      else
10      {
11          Node parent;
12          var temp = root;
13
14          while (true)
15          {
16              parent = temp;
17
18              if (value < temp.Value)
19              {
20                  temp = temp.Left;
21
22                  if (temp is null)
23                  {
24                      parent.Left = newNode;
25                      newNode.Parent = parent;
26                      return;
27                  }
28              }
29              else
30              {
31                  temp = temp.Right;
32
33                  if (temp is null)
34                  {
35                      parent.Right = newNode;
```

```
36                      newNode.Parent = parent;
37                      return;
38                  }
39              }
40          }
41      }
42  }
```

Now, we can add the **Iterator** object for our sorted binary tree collection:

```
1   namespace Iterator_Demo;
2
3   internal class SortedBinaryTreeIterator : IIterator
4   {
5       private readonly SortedBinaryTreeCollection aggregate;
6       private Node? current;
7
8       public SortedBinaryTreeIterator(SortedBinaryTreeColle\
9   ction aggregate)
10      {
11          this.aggregate = aggregate;
12          current = null;
13      }
14
15      public int GetCurrent()
16      {
17          return current.Value;
18      }
19  }
```

We will then add the following public method to it to allow us to traverse the tree from left to right:

```
 1  public bool MoveNext()
 2  {
 3      if (current is null)
 4      {
 5          current = aggregate.GetFirst();
 6          return true;
 7      }
 8
 9      if (current.Right is not null)
10      {
11          current = current.Right;
12
13          while (true)
14          {
15              if (current.Left is null)
16              {
17                  break;
18              }
19
20              current = current.Left;
21          }
22
23          return true;
24      }
25      else
26      {
27          var originalValue = current.Value;
28
29          while (true)
30          {
31              if (current.Parent is not null)
32              {
33                  current = current.Parent;
34
35                  if (current.Value > originalValue)
```

```
36                    {
37                        return true;
38                    }
39                }
40                else
41                {
42                    return false;
43                }
44            }
45        }
46  }
```

So, the consumer of this **Iterator** doesn't have to know anything about the tree structure. All it cares about is that, while there are still items in the tree, it can retrieve them all one by one.

Now, we can examine the differences in output of our two **Iterator** objects. To do so, we will replace the content of Program.cs file with the following:

```
1   using Iterator_Demo;
2
3   var listOfValues = new List<int>()
4   {
5       8, 19, 25, 2, 4, 7, 32, 90, 3, 1
6   };
7
8   var listAggregate = new ListAggregate();
9
10  foreach (var value in listOfValues)
11  {
12      listAggregate.Insert(value);
13  }
14
15  var listIterator = listAggregate.CreateIterator();
16
```

```
17    Console.WriteLine("Values from List Iterator:");
18
19    while (listIterator.MoveNext())
20    {
21        Console.Write($"{listIterator.GetCurrent()}, ");
22    }
23
24    var treeAggregate = new SortedBinaryTreeCollection();
25
26    foreach (var value in listOfValues)
27    {
28        treeAggregate.Insert(value);
29    }
30
31    var treeIterator = treeAggregate.CreateIterator();
32
33    Console.WriteLine("");
34    Console.WriteLine("Values from Binary Tree Iterator:");
35
36    while (treeIterator.MoveNext())
37    {
38        Console.Write($"{treeIterator.GetCurrent()}, ");
39    }
40
41    Console.ReadKey();
```

And, as we can see in the screenshot below, even though we have used identical inputs for both of the collection types, the collection inside ListAggregate was identical to the input collection, while the collection inside SortedBinaryTreeCollection was returned sorted. And this is because the former **Aggregate** used just a plain List, while the latter used a sorted binary tree, which was traversed from left to right.

```
Values from List Iterator:
8, 19, 25, 2, 4, 7, 32, 90, 3, 1,
Values from Binary Tree Iterator:
1, 2, 3, 4, 7, 8, 19, 25, 32, 90,
```

Figure 38.2 - Two iterators showing different results

This concludes our example of the Iterator design pattern. Let's now summarize all its key benefits.

Benefits of using Iterator

The main benefits of using Iterator design pattern are as follows:

- Single responsibility principle is well maintained, as maintaining the collection and iterating through it are performed by different objects.
- If you are dealing with complex data structures, the Iterator design pattern significantly simplifies this process.
- Because you can create more than one **Iterator** from each **Aggregate**, you can iterate through the same collection in parallel.

And now let's examine some things that you should watch out for while using the Iterator pattern.

Caveats of using Iterator

If we go back to our ListAggregate, you will see that we have hardly added any value to it. The object merely encapsulates an inbuilt List data type. And this data type has its own **Iterator**, which, in the language of C# system library is called Enumerator.

And this demonstrates the first problem with using the Iterator design pattern. If you are dealing with simple collections, it would be better to just deal with them directly. If you apply Iterator design pattern in such a situation, you will only make your code more complicated without adding any value at all. So, you should only reserve this design pattern for complex collection types.

But even while dealing with complex collection types, it is worth checking whether it wouldn't be more efficient to just traverse the collection directly. Even though the Iterator design pattern allows you to provide a convenient interface that enables the consuming client to traverse the collection in one direction, it could be that for certain collection types traversing it in one direction wouldn't be the most appropriate or the most efficient thing to do.

39. Mediator

Mediator is a design pattern where one object facilitates communication between multiple other objects. It's analogous to air traffic control, which acts as a mediator between different flights. Planes can talk to the air traffic control, which then delivers relevant information to other planes. But planes don't talk to each other directly.

Mediator design pattern can be summarized as follows:

- There is a **Mediator** object, the role of which is to hold a list of **Participants** and facilitate communication between them.
- There are multiple **Participant** objects, which can be of completely different types.
- When a **Participant** wants to send a message to another **Participant**, it sends the message to **Mediator**.
- Based on some parameter that identifies the recipient, **Mediator** sends the message to an appropriate **Participant**.

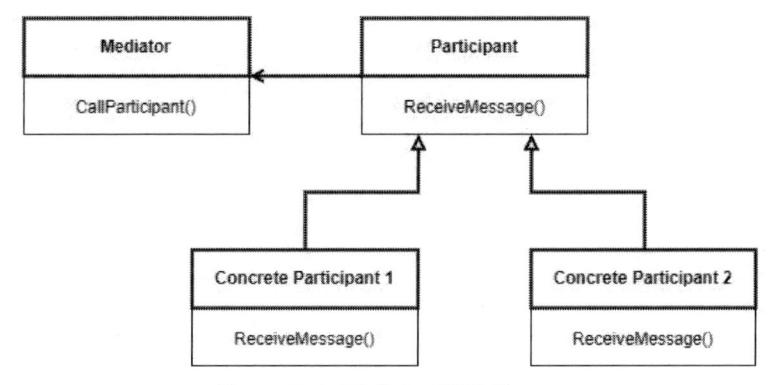

Figure 39.1 - Mediator UML diagram

We will now go through an example implementation of Mediator. The complete solution can be found via the link below:

https://github.com/fiodarsazanavets/design-patterns-in-csharp/tree/main/Behavioral_Patterns/Mediator

Prerequisites

In order to be able to implement the code samples below, you need the following installed on your machine:

- .NET 6 SDK (or newer)
- A suitable IDE or a code editor (Visual Studio, Visual Studio Code, JetBrains Rider)

Mediator implementation example

As in all other examples, we will create a console application project. In this example, we will be building a system that represents a peer-to-peer computer network. Each device in the network will be a **Participant**. And the object representing the network will act as **Mediator**.

First, we will define the common interface that each **Participant** will implement. The interface will look as follows:

```
1   namespace Mediator_Demo;
2
3   internal interface IParticipant
4   {
5       void SendCommand(string receiver, string command);
6       void ReceiveCommand(string sender, string command);
7   }
```

Then, we will define the interface for the **Mediator**:

```
1   namespace Mediator_Demo;
2
3   internal interface IMediator
4   {
5       void Register(string key, IParticipant participant);
6       void SendCommand(string receiver, string sender, stri\
7   ng command);
8   }
```

Because different **Participant** types will share some common functionality, we will also add the following abstract class that each **Participant** will inherit from:

```
1   namespace Mediator_Demo;
2
3   internal abstract class Participant : IParticipant
4   {
5       private IMediator mediator;
6
7       protected string key;
8
9       public Participant(string key, IMediator mediator)
10      {
11          this.key = key;
12          this.mediator = mediator;
```

```
13        }
14
15        public virtual void SendCommand(string receiver, stri\
16   ng command)
17        {
18            mediator.SendCommand(receiver, key, command);
19        }
20
21        public virtual void ReceiveCommand(string sender, str\
22   ing command)
23        {
24            Console.WriteLine($"Executing command {command} i\
25   ssued by {sender}.");
26        }
27   }
```

As you can see, when the SendCommand method is called, the call gets passed to the **Mediator**.

Now, we can add some concrete **Participant** implementations. We will first add the following class that represents a desktop computer:

```
1    namespace Mediator_Demo;
2
3    internal class DesktopComputer : Participant
4    {
5        public DesktopComputer(string key,
6        IMediator mediator) : base(key, mediator)
7        {
8        }
9
10       public override void SendCommand(string receiver, str\
11   ing command)
12       {
13           Console.WriteLine($"Sending {command} command to \
14   {receiver}.");
```

```
15            base.SendCommand(receiver, command);
16        }
17
18        public override void ReceiveCommand(string sender, st\
19   ring command)
20        {
21            Console.Write($"Desktop computer {key} received a\
22    command. ");
23            base.ReceiveCommand(sender, command);
24        }
25   }
```

Then, we will add the following class that represents a server:

```
1    namespace Mediator_Demo;
2
3    internal class Server : Participant
4    {
5        public Server(string key,
6        IMediator mediator) : base(key, mediator)
7        {
8        }
9
10       public override void SendCommand(string receiver, str\
11   ing command)
12       {
13           Console.WriteLine($"Server has issued {command} c\
14   ommand to {receiver}.");
15           base.SendCommand(receiver, command);
16       }
17
18       public override void ReceiveCommand(string sender, st\
19   ring command)
20       {
21           Console.Write($"Server {key} received a command. \
```

```
");
        base.ReceiveCommand(sender, command);
    }
}
```

The logic in both of these **Participant** types is similar. But it's different enough to make them distinct.

Next, we will add the following **Mediator** implementation:

```
namespace Mediator_Demo;

internal class NetworkMediator : IMediator
{
    private Dictionary<string, IParticipant> participants;

    public NetworkMediator()
    {
        participants = new Dictionary<string, IParticipan\
t>();
    }

    public void Register(string key, IParticipant partici\
pant)
    {
        participants[key] = participant;
    }

    public void SendCommand(string receiver, string sende\
r, string command)
    {
        if (participants.ContainsKey(receiver))
        {
            participants[receiver].ReceiveCommand(sender,\
 command);
        }
```

```
27        }
28    }
```

In here, we register all **Participant** instances in a dictionary. Dictionary key is the identifier that allows each **Participant** to tell the **Mediator** which **Participant** the message needs to be sent to.

Finally, we will bring it all together by replacing the content of the Program.cs file with the following:

```
1   using Mediator_Demo;
2
3   var networkMediator = new NetworkMediator();
4   var desktopComputer = new DesktopComputer("computer-1", n\
5   etworkMediator);
6   var server = new Server("server-1", networkMediator);
7
8   networkMediator.Register("computer-1", desktopComputer);
9   networkMediator.Register("server-1", server);
10
11  desktopComputer.SendCommand("server-1", "reboot");
12  server.SendCommand("computer-1", "trigger-updates");
13
14  Console.ReadKey();
```

And, as we can see from the screenshot below, we were able to register different **Participant** instances inside the **Mediator** object and get them to communicate with each other via the **Mediator**.

Figure 39.2 - The results of using Mediator

Let's now summarize the main benefits of using the Mediator design pattern.

Benefits of using Mediator

The main benefits of using the Mediator design pattern are as follows:

- It significantly reduces coupling between objects, as none of the **Participants** call each other directly.
- Both the single responsibility principle and the open-closed principle are well enforced.

Perhaps there is only one caveat with the Mediator design pattern. And this is what we will have a look at next.

Caveats of using Mediator

The main danger with using the Mediator design pattern is that, if you have to deal with many different **Participant** types, your **Mediator** object can easily evolve into a God object - the antipattern that is opposite to the single responsibility principle. Therefore, while using Mediator, it's often worth applying other design patterns inside the **Mediator** object to ensure that each individual piece of logic is handled by its own component.

40. Memento

Memento is a design pattern that is used specifically for storing intermediate states of some data, so the actions can be undone and the state can be reverted.

Memento design pattern can be summarized as follows:

- There is an **Originator** object, which acts as the origin of the data that can change its state at will.
- There is a **Memento** object, which represents a single snapshot of the data.
- **Originator** object can generate a new instance of **Memento** when some action is performed, or accept an instance of **Memento** to reset its data.
- There's also a **Caretaker** object, which stores a collection of **Memento** objects in a stack. This stack represents the history of changes.
- The **Caretaker** object also coordinates the history of changes with the **Originator** and allows the consumer to undo the actions.

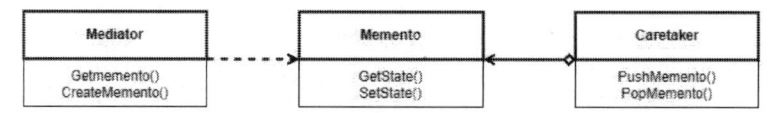

Figure 40.1 - Memento UML diagram

We will now go through an example implementation of Memento. The complete solution can be found via the link below:

https://github.com/fiodarsazanavets/design-patterns-in-csharp/tree/main/Behavioral_Patterns/Memento

Prerequisites

In order to be able to implement the code samples below, you need the following installed on your machine:

- .NET 6 SDK (or newer)
- A suitable IDE or a code editor (Visual Studio, Visual Studio Code, JetBrains Rider)

Memento implementation example

After creating a project based on a console application template, we will add the following interface to it, which will represent the public methods available on the **Memento** object:

```
namespace Memento_Demo;

internal interface IMemento
{
    string GetState();
    DateTimeOffset GetCreatedDate();
}
```

The concrete **Memento** implementation will look as follows:

```csharp
namespace Memento_Demo;

internal class TextEditorMemento : IMemento
{
    private readonly string state;
    private readonly DateTimeOffset created;

    public TextEditorMemento(string state)
    {
        this.state = state;
        created = DateTimeOffset.Now;
    }

    public string GetState()
    {
        return state;
    }

    public DateTimeOffset GetCreatedDate()
    {
        return created;
    }
}
```

Because this object is only ever meant to represent an immutable snapshot, both its state and the timestamp are read-only. They only get populated via the class constructor.

We will now add our **Originator** object. This will be a class that represents a text editor. In this text editor, you can update text at any point. When you save text, a **Memento** object is generated. Also, at any point, the internal state can be restored to one of the previous snapshots by passing a **Memento** object into the SetState method.

```csharp
namespace Memento_Demo;

internal class TextEditor
{
    private string state;

    public TextEditor()
    {
        state = string.Empty;
    }

    public string GetCurrentText()
    {
            return state;
    }

    public void UpdateText(string updatedText)
    {
        state = updatedText;
    }

    public IMemento Save()
    {
        Console.WriteLine("Saving state.");
        return new TextEditorMemento(state);
    }

    public void SetState(IMemento memento)
    {
        state = memento.GetState();
        Console.WriteLine($"Restored the state from the s\
napshot created at {memento.GetCreatedDate()}.");
    }
}
```

Next, we will add a **Caretaker** object. This object stores the history of previous **Memento** objects on a stack and coordinates this history with the **Originator** object.

```csharp
namespace Memento_Demo;

internal class Caretaker
{
    private TextEditor textEditor;
    private Stack<IMemento> history;

    public Caretaker(TextEditor textEditor)
    {
        this.textEditor = textEditor;
        history = new Stack<IMemento>();
    }

    public void Backup()
    {
        history.Push(textEditor.Save());
    }

    public void Revert()
    {
        Console.WriteLine("Restoring a snapshot from history.");

        if (history.Count == 0)
        {
            Console.WriteLine("No snapshots to restore.");
            return;
        }

        textEditor.SetState(history.Pop());
    }
}
```

Finally, we will replace the content of the Program.cs file with the following. We create some **Memento** snapshots and see what happens if we attempt to revert them.

```
1  using Memento_Demo;
2
3  var textEditor = new TextEditor();
4  var caretaker = new Caretaker(textEditor);
5
6  textEditor.UpdateText("Original text.");
7  Console.WriteLine($"Updated text to '{textEditor.GetCurre\
8  ntText()}'.");
9  caretaker.Backup();
10 textEditor.UpdateText("First edit.");
11 Console.WriteLine($"Updated text to '{textEditor.GetCurre\
12 ntText()}'.");
13 caretaker.Backup();
14 textEditor.UpdateText("Second edit.");
15 Console.WriteLine($"Updated text to '{textEditor.GetCurre\
16 ntText()}'.");
17 caretaker.Backup();
18
19 textEditor.UpdateText("Third edit.");
20 Console.WriteLine($"Updated text to '{textEditor.GetCurre\
21 ntText()}'.");
22
23 caretaker.Revert();
24 Console.WriteLine($"Reverted text to '{textEditor.GetCurr\
25 entText()}'.");
26 caretaker.Revert();
27 Console.WriteLine($"Reverted text to '{textEditor.GetCurr\
28 entText()}'.");
29 caretaker.Revert();
30 Console.WriteLine($"Reverted text to '{textEditor.GetCurr\
31 entText()}'.");
32
```

```
33    Console.ReadKey();
```

And, as we can see from the screenshot below, we are able to revert the text in the text editor to its previous state.

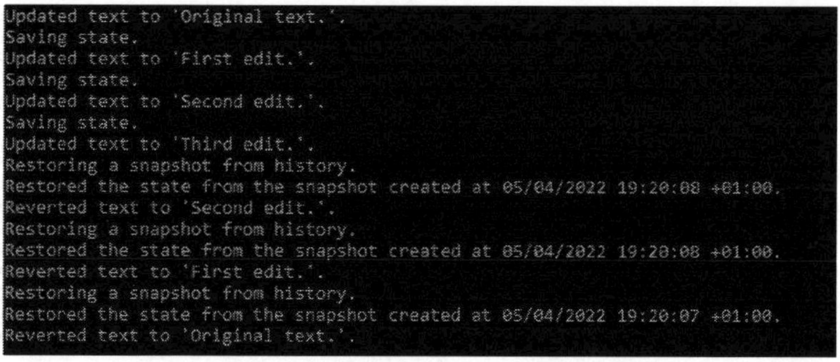

Figure 40.2 - Undoing actions by using Memento

Now, let's summarize the benefits of using the Memento design pattern.

Benefits of using Memento

Memento design pattern gives you the following key benefits:

- Because snapshot **Memento** objects are separate from the internal state of the **Originator**, you can get them to store only as much or as little information as possible.
- The history of changes is easy to construct and revert.
- Because there is a separate **Caretaker** object involved, the single responsibility principle is well maintained.

But, as effective as Memento design pattern is for enabling *undo* action, there are some things to look out for while using it. And this is what we will have a look at next.

Caveats of using Memento

The main thing to look out for while using Memento design pattern is that your **Memento** stack doesn't consume too much memory, which can happen if the history grows too large. You can mitigate this by making sure that you only save those elements of the state that you definitely need to keep track of and nothing else. You can add some rules that would remove older entries in the history. Or perhaps you can even combine Memento with the Flyweight design pattern, saving common states in shared objects.

Also, in some situations, the **Originator** object may complete its lifecycle and get out of scope of the program. In this case, the history of its snapshots will serve no purpose, while it will still be occupying the memory. To mitigate against this, you will need to keep the track of the **Originator's** lifecycle inside the **Caretaker** object and clear the history when appropriate.

41. Observer

Observer is a design pattern that facilitates communication between objects via publication and subscription model. When using this pattern, objects can subscribe to each other, so they would get notified when specific events are triggered. They can also unsubscribe from each other at any point.

Observer design pattern can be summarized as follows:

- **Subject** or **Publisher** is an object that emits some events
- **Observer** or **Subscriber** is an object that can subscribe to the **Subject**, so it can receive notifications when a specific event occurs.
- **Subject** exposes methods that allow **Observer** objects to subscribe to or unsubscribe from it.
- **Subject** maintains internal list of all **Observer** objects that are subscribed to it.

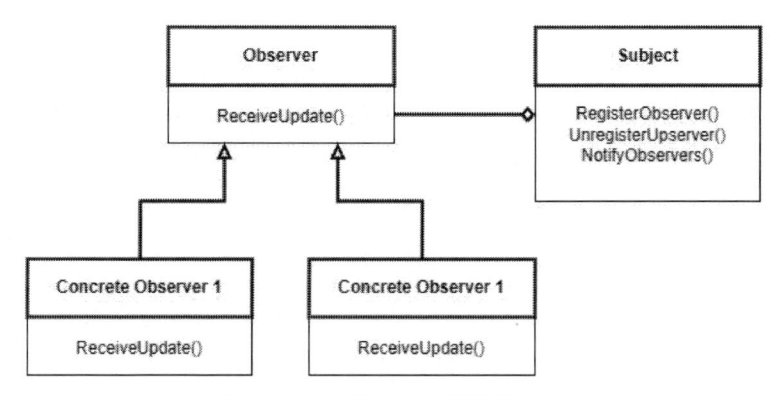

Figure 41.1 - Observer UML diagram

We will now go through an example implementation of Observer. The complete solution can be found via the link below:

https://github.com/fiodarsazanavets/design-patterns-in-csharp/tree/main/Behavioral_Patterns/Observer

Prerequisites

In order to be able to implement the code samples below, you need the following installed on your machine:

- .NET 6 SDK (or newer)
- A suitable IDE or a code editor (Visual Studio, Visual Studio Code, JetBrains Rider)

Observer implementation example

In this example, you will see how easily **Observer** objects can subscribe to events and unsubscribe from them. As in all other examples, we will use the console application template for this demo.

First, we will add an interface for our **Subject**. This interface would allow **Observer** objects to subscribe and unsubscribe. We can also use this interface to notify all the **Observer** objects that are subscribed to the **Subject**.

And don't worry about the compilation error related to `IObserver` not being present. We will add it later.

```
1  namespace Observer_Demo;
2
3  internal interface ISubject
4  {
5      string Name { get; }
6      void Subscribe(IObserver observer);
7      void Unsubscribe(IObserver observer);
8      void Notify(string message);
9  }
```

And this will be the interface for our **Observer** objects. It allows each of these objects to be notified by a specific **Subject**.

```
1  namespace Observer_Demo;
2
3  internal interface IObserver
4  {
5      void Update(ISubject subject, string message);
6  }
```

Next, we will add an implementation of our **Subject**. Because a **Subject** can also be referred to as a **Publisher**, we have called our class Publisher.

```
1   namespace Observer_Demo;
2
3   internal class Publisher : ISubject
4   {
5       private string name;
6       private List<IObserver> observers;
7
8       public Publisher(string name)
9       {
10          this.name = name;
11          observers = new List<IObserver>();
```

```
12      }
13
14      public string Name => name;
15
16      public void Subscribe(IObserver observer)
17      {
18          observers.Add(observer);
19      }
20
21      public void Unsubscribe(IObserver observer)
22      {
23          observers.Remove(observer);
24      }
25
26      public void Notify(string message)
27      {
28          foreach (var observer in observers)
29          {
30              observer.Update(this, message);
31          }
32      }
33  }
```

This class has a list of **Observer** objects. When something calls the Notify method, every object of this list gets updated. Adding a new **Observer** object to the list is done via the Subscribe method. Removing an **Observer** from the list is done via the Unsubscribe method.

Now, we will add an implementation of our **Observer**. As an **Observer** object is also referred to as a **Subscriber**, we have called our class Subscriber.

```
1   namespace Observer_Demo;
2
3   internal class Subscriber : IObserver
4   {
5       private string name;
6
7       public Subscriber(string name)
8       {
9           this.name = name;
10      }
11
12      public void Update(ISubject subject, string message)
13      {
14          Console.WriteLine($"'{message}' message received \
15  from {subject.Name} by {name}.");
16      }
17  }
```

Now, we will bring it all together. We will replace the content of Program.cs file with the following code:

```
1   using Observer_Demo;
2
3   var publisher = new Publisher("Message Hub");
4   var subscriber1 = new Subscriber("First Subscriber");
5   var subscriber2 = new Subscriber("Second Subscriber");
6   var subscriber3 = new Subscriber("Third Subscriber");
7
8   Console.WriteLine("Adding the first and the second subscr\
9   ibers to the publisher.");
10  publisher.Subscribe(subscriber1);
11  publisher.Subscribe(subscriber2);
12
13  Console.WriteLine("Notifying subscribers.");
14  publisher.Notify("Sequence initiated.");
```

```
15
16  Console.WriteLine("Removing the first subscriber.");
17  publisher.Unsubscribe(subscriber1);
18
19  Console.WriteLine("Adding the third subscriber.");
20  publisher.Subscribe(subscriber3);
21
22  Console.WriteLine("Notifying subscribers.");
23  publisher.Notify("Update received from the server.");
24
25  Console.ReadKey();
```

In here, we have three **Subscriber** objects. First, we will only add the first and the second **Subscribers** to the **Subject**. Then, we notify all of the subscribers that are listed by our **Subject**. Then, we remove the first subscriber and add the third one, after which we notify the subscribers again.

And, as the following screenshot shows, all the correct **Observer** objects get notified:

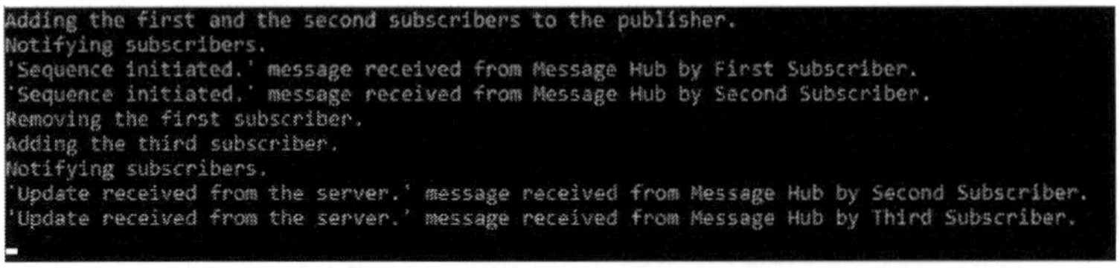

Figure 41.2 - Subscribing and unsubscribing by using Observer

This concluded the overview of the Observer design pattern. Let's now summarize its main benefits.

Benefits of using Observer

The key benefits of using the Observer design pattern are as follows:

- The relationships between objects can be established and removed at runtime.
- Each object has its own pre-defined role, so the single responsibility principle is well maintained.

And now let's have a look at the caveats of using the Observer design pattern that you should be familiar with.

Caveats of using Observer

Perhaps the only caveat of using the Observer design pattern is that the subscribed objects don't get updated at the same time and there is no guarantee in what order they will be updated. In most cases, it's not a problem. But it might be an issue in some scenarios.

Also, if you are building a real-life distributed application, having a proper publisher/subscription (pub/sub) system might be more appropriate than using the Observer design pattern. But still, even if you do use such a system, being familiar with how the Observer design pattern works will automatically make you understand the key principles behind any pub/sub system.

42. State

State is a design pattern that allows developers to change behavior of an object depending on what state the object is in. The public interface of the object, however, remains the same.

You can think of it as being analogous to a smartphone. When the phone is in a locked state, pressing the Home button brings up a prompt for the unlock PIN. However, if the phone is already unlocked, pressing the same button takes you to the home screen. It's the same button. But it behaves differently if your device is in a different state. And the same thing can be done in the code.

State design pattern can be summarized as follows:

- There is a **Context** object, which contains the **State** interface.
- **State** interface would have multiple implementations, each with its own behavior.
- The role of **Context** object is to trigger specific public methods in the current **State** implementation and to allow **State** implementation to be changed.
- **State** implementations are never manipulated directly by an external client. Only **Context** object is called directly by outer code.
- However, the outer code can instruct the **Context** to change the concrete implementation of **State** object inside itself.

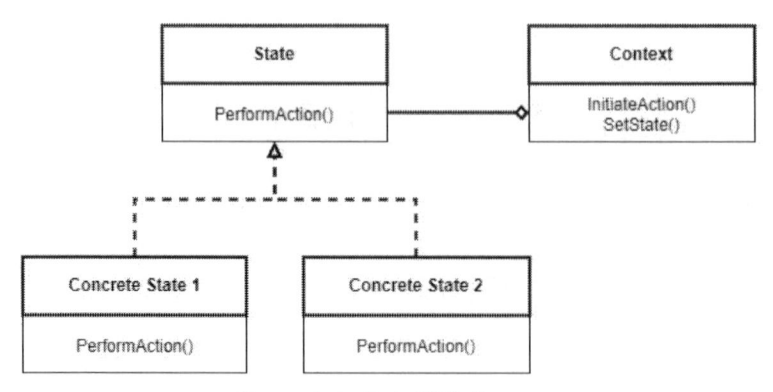

Figure 42.1 - State UML diagram

We will now go through an example implementation of State. The complete solution can be found via the link below:

https://github.com/fiodarsazanavets/design-patterns-in-csharp/tree/main/Behavioral_Patterns/State

Prerequisites

In order to be able to implement the code samples below, you need the following installed on your machine:

- .NET 6 SDK (or newer)
- A suitable IDE or a code editor (Visual Studio, Visual Studio Code, JetBrains Rider)

State implementation example

We will create a console application project, which will mimic the basic operation of a smartphone. All we need for the demonstration purposes is to show how the smartphone's Home button behaves differently when its state changes.

First, we will need to add the following interface for its **State**. Regardless of what state the phone is in, the user will still be able to press the Home button. And the interface reflects this.

```
1  namespace State_Demo;
2
3  internal interface IMobilePhoneState
4  {
5      void PressHomeButton();
6  }
```

Next, we will add a concrete implementation of the **State**. In this implementation, pressing the Home button brings up the screen unlock prompt.

```
1   namespace State_Demo;
2
3   internal class LockedScreenState : IMobilePhoneState
4   {
5       public void PressHomeButton()
6       {
7           Console.WriteLine("Please enter screen unlock PIN\
8   .");
9       }
10  }
```

After this, we will add another **State** implementation. In this case, pressing the Home button opens the home screen.

```
namespace State_Demo;

internal class UnlockedScreenState : IMobilePhoneState
{
    public void PressHomeButton()
    {
        Console.WriteLine("Home screen has been opened.");
    }
}
```

Next, we will add our **Context** object. This object holds one **State** implementation at a time. The clients of this object can change the **State** and can trigger PressHomeButton method on the **State**.

```
namespace State_Demo;

internal class MobilePhoneContext
{
    IMobilePhoneState state;

    public MobilePhoneContext()
    {
        state = new LockedScreenState();
    }

    public void ChangeState(IMobilePhoneState state)
    {
        this.state = state;
    }

    public void PressHomeButton()
    {
        state.PressHomeButton();
    }
}
```

Now, we will bring it all together to see how the behavior changes when we change the **State**. To do so, we will replace the content of the Program.cs file with the following:

```
1  using State_Demo;
2
3  var phone = new MobilePhoneContext();
4
5  Console.WriteLine("Pressing home button.");
6  phone.PressHomeButton();
7
8  Console.WriteLine("Changing the phone state to unlocked."\
9  );
10 phone.ChangeState(new UnlockedScreenState());
11
12 Console.WriteLine("Pressing home button.");
13 phone.PressHomeButton();
14
15 Console.ReadKey();
```

And here is the output of this program:

```
Pressing home button.
Please enter screen unlock PIN.
Changing the phone state to unlocked.
Pressing home button.
Home screen has been opened.
```

Figure 42.2 - **Demonstration of changed behavior due to changed State**

We will now summarize the benefits of using the State design pattern.

Benefits of using State

So, the key benefits of using the State design pattern can be summarized as follows:

- There is a clear separation between the types of the behavior that should occur in different scenarios, so the single responsibility principle is well maintained.
- The open-closed principle is well implemented, as you can easily add new behaviors to the existing functionality by simply adding new states.
- Complex conditions are eliminated from the code.

Now, let's have a look at the situations where the State design pattern wouldn't perhaps be the best solution.

Caveats of using State

If you are working with some objects where the state can change, but these changes occur infrequently and don't require complex conditional logic, then perhaps the State design pattern will only overcomplicate things without adding a lot of value. If you can still write clean code that can be easily maintained and tested without using this design pattern, then it might be an indication that this design pattern is needed.

However, if you are working with objects where the state is expected to change fairly frequently and/or such change would require relatively complex code, then it is indeed an ideal scenario for using the State design pattern.

43. Strategy

Strategy design pattern allows you to write maintainable code in situations where conditional logic needs to be applied. Instead of placing a specific piece of logic under a specific condition in the code, you would move each of such pieces of logic into its own class. All of these classes would implement exactly the same interface. So, all you would have to do in your if or switch statement is pick up a specific implementation of this interface that is appropriate to a specific condition. Then, all you have to do is just execute the action method to trigger this logic.

Below, we will examine some very clear benefits of this approach. But for now, let's summarize the Strategy design pattern:

- There is a **Strategy** interface that defines the action method that may or may not return some data.
- There are multiple **Concrete Strategy** implementations.
- There is a **Context** object, which encapsulates **Strategy** interface.
- The **Context** object allows the calling code to set its internal **Strategy** field to a **Concrete Strategy** implementation.
- The **Context** object allows the calling code to execute the action method on the current implementation of **Strategy**.
- The **Concrete Strategy** implementation is set on the **Context** based on some conditional logic.

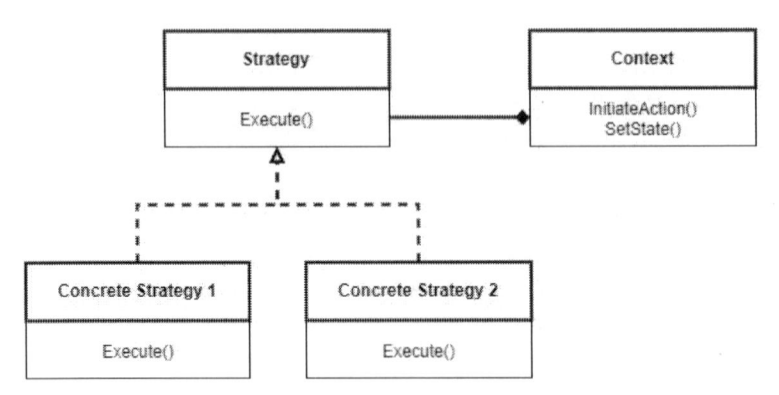

Figure 43.1 - Strategy UML diagram

We will now go through an example implementation of Strategy. The complete solution can be found via the link below:

https://github.com/fiodarsazanavets/design-patterns-in-csharp/tree/main/Behavioral_Patterns/Strategy

Prerequisites

In order to be able to implement the code samples below, you need the following installed on your machine:

- .NET 6 SDK (or newer)
- A suitable IDE or a code editor (Visual Studio, Visual Studio Code, JetBrains Rider)

Strategy implementation example

We will be building an application that is able to play audio on both Linux and Windows operating systems. It will be similar to the application that we have built while looking at the Factory Method design pattern. But this time, instead of conditionally returning an appropriate player, we will conditionally trigger a one-off playback.

And this demonstrates the fundamental difference between the Strategy and the Factory Method design patterns, as it's not uncommon for people to confuse the two. The intention behind the Factory Method is to return a long-lived object that can be then reused. The intention behind the Strategy is to execute a one-off action there and then.

We will start by creating a console application project. Then, we will add the following interface, which will represent our **Strategy**.

```
1  namespace Strategy_Demo;
2
3  internal interface IPlayerStrategy
4  {
5      Task Play(string fileName);
6  }
```

We will then add a concrete implementation of this interface that is capable of playing audio on Linux machines:

```
1   using System.Diagnostics;
2
3   namespace Strategy_Demo;
4
5   public class LinuxPlayerStrategy : IPlayerStrategy
6   {
7       public Task Play(string fileName)
8       {
9           StartBashProcess($"mpg123 -q '{fileName}'");
10          return Task.CompletedTask;
11      }
12
13      private void StartBashProcess(string command)
```

```
        {
            var escapedArgs = command.Replace("\"", "\\\"");

            var process = new Process()
            {
                StartInfo = new ProcessStartInfo
                {
                    FileName = "/bin/bash",
                    Arguments = $"-c \"{escapedArgs}\"",
                    RedirectStandardOutput = true,
                    RedirectStandardInput = true,
                    UseShellExecute = false,
                    CreateNoWindow = true,
                }
            };

            process.Start();
        }
}
```

And then we will add the following implementation that will allow us to play audio on Windows:

```
using System.Runtime.InteropServices;
using System.Text;

namespace Strategy_Demo;

internal class WindowsPlayerStrategy : IPlayerStrategy
{
    [DllImport("winmm.dll")]
    private static extern int mciSendString(string comman\
d, StringBuilder stringReturn, int returnLength, IntPtr h\
wndCallback);

```

```
13      public Task Play(string fileName)
14      {
15          var sb = new StringBuilder();
16          var result = mciSendString($"Play {fileName}", sb\
17   , 1024 * 1024, IntPtr.Zero);
18          Console.WriteLine(result);
19          return Task.CompletedTask;
20      }
21  }
```

Now, we will add our **Context** object, which will be as follows:

```
1   namespace Strategy_Demo;
2
3   internal class PlayerContext
4   {
5       private IPlayerStrategy strategy;
6
7       public void SetStrategy(IPlayerStrategy strategy)
8       {
9           this.strategy = strategy;
10      }
11
12      public Task Play(string fileName)
13      {
14          return strategy.Play(fileName);
15      }
16  }
```

And now, we will replace the content of Program.cs class with the following:

```
1   using System.Runtime.InteropServices;
2   using Strategy_Demo;
3
4   var context = new PlayerContext();
5
6   if (RuntimeInformation.IsOSPlatform(OSPlatform.Windows))
7       context.SetStrategy(new WindowsPlayerStrategy());
8   else if (RuntimeInformation.IsOSPlatform(OSPlatform.Linux\
9   ))
10      context.SetStrategy(new LinuxPlayerStrategy());
11  else
12      throw new Exception("Only Linux and Windows operating\
13   systems are supported.");
14
15  Console.WriteLine("Please specify the path to the file to\
16   play.");
17  var filePath = Console.ReadLine() ?? string.Empty;
18
19  context.Play(filePath);
20
21  Console.ReadKey();
```

We check which operating system we are running the program on. If it's either Linux or Windows, we set the appropriate **Strategy** implementation inside our **Context**. And then we execute the action on our **Context**, which triggers the behavior specific to the current **Strategy** implementation.

And this concludes the overview of the Strategy design pattern. Let's now summarize its benefits.

Benefits of using Strategy

The main benefits of using the Strategy design pattern are as follows:

- It reduces complex conditional logic from the code, as each type of behavior is handled by its own strategy.
- You can easily swap algorithms during runtime.
- Because the **Context** retains its **Strategy**, you don't have to execute conditional logic every time you need to execute the action.
- Both the single responsibility principle and the open-closed principle are well maintained.

But, as good as the Strategy pattern is, it might still be not appropriate in some situations. Let's examine why.

Caveats of using Strategy

As with the State design pattern, using Strategy might overcomplicate things in scenarios where the conditional logic isn't too complicated to begin with. In these situations, it might be more appropriate to just apply the conditional logic directly.

Likewise, all modern programming languages, including C#, have components that allow you to provide method templates (delegates, anonymous actions, etc.) without having to have interfaces and implementations. And in some situations, it would be more appropriate to use these language features instead of having a whole bunch of extra classes and interfaces.

Otherwise, Strategy is still a useful design pattern and there are many scenarios where it will prove helpful.

44. Template Method

Template Method design pattern is all about using a combination of concrete and abstract logic inside an abstract class to create multiple concrete instances of it. Template Method would be defined inside an abstract class, so it cannot be used directly. It will have to be overridden by a concrete implementation of such a class.

It's not to be confused with using interfaces or pure abstract classes. What makes the Template Method unique is that some pieces of logic inside of it are already concrete. Typically, this is achieved by having a concrete public method that calls various protected methods. However, some or all of these protected methods would be abstract, which makes the behavior of the class unique to each of its implementations.

Template Method design pattern can be summarized as follows:

- There is an abstract class with a non-abstract public method that calls one or more abstract protected methods.
- Any concrete implementation of this class will need to override the abstract protected methods, giving them implementation-specific behavior.
- As a result, the overall behavior of the public method that calls those abstract methods will be unique based on implementation.

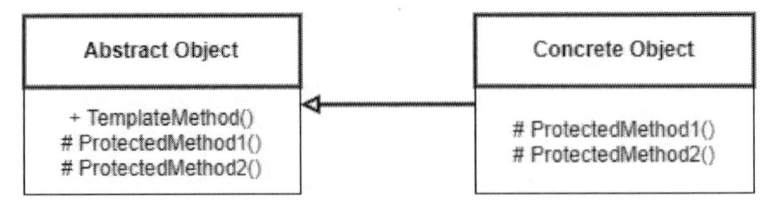

Figure 44.1 - Template Method UML diagram

We will now go through an example implementation of Template Method. The complete solution can be found via the link below:

https://github.com/fiodarsazanavets/design-patterns-in-csharp/tree/main/Behavioral_Patterns/Template-Method

Prerequisites

In order to be able to implement the code samples below, you need the following installed on your machine:

- .NET 6 SDK (or newer)
- A suitable IDE or a code editor (Visual Studio, Visual Studio Code, JetBrains Rider)

Template Method implementation example

In this example, we will be building an application that is capable of converting text from one format to another. We will use the console application as our project type. And the first thing that we will do is add the following abstract class, which contains the template method:

```csharp
using System.Text;
using System.Text.RegularExpressions;

namespace Template_Method_Demo;

internal abstract class AbstractTextToHtmlConverter
{
    protected string ProcessParagraphs(string text)
    {
        var paragraphs = Regex.Split(text, @"(\r\n?|\n)")
                            .Where(p => p.Any(char.IsLetter\
OrDigit));

        var sb = new StringBuilder();

        foreach (var paragraph in paragraphs)
        {
            if (paragraph.Length == 0)
                continue;

            sb.AppendLine($"<p>{paragraph}</p>");
        }

        sb.AppendLine("<br/>");
        return sb.ToString();
    }

    protected abstract string ApplyPostProcessing(string \
text);

    public string ConvertText(string text)
    {
        text = ProcessParagraphs(text);
        return ApplyPostProcessing(text);
    }
```

```
36  }
```

As you can see, we have a public method called `ConvertText`, which has some pre-defined logic. This method calls two protected methods: `ProcessParagraphs` and `ApplyPostProcessing`. The former method also has some pre-defined content. However, the latter one is abstract, so it can have any implementation.

What we are doing in this class is converting some basic text to HTML. Let's now create a class that inherits from this abstract class. We will call it `BasicTextToHtmlConverter`. In this implementation, there is no real post-processing happening. We are just returning the input text without any changes.

```
namespace Template_Method_Demo;

internal class BasicTextToHtmlConverter : AbstractTextToH\
tmlConverter
{
    protected override string ApplyPostProcessing(string \
text)
    {
        return text;
    }
}
```

And then we will add another implementation of this abstract class, which assumes that the input text is Markdown (MD). In this case, the post-processing step will search for MD markers in the text and replace them with appropriate HTML tags.

```
namespace Template_Method_Demo;

internal class MdToHtmlConverter : AbstractTextToHtmlConv\
erter
{
    private readonly Dictionary<string, (string, string)>\
 tagsToReplace;

    public MdToHtmlConverter()
    {
        tagsToReplace = new Dictionary<string, (string, s\
tring)>
        {
            { "**", ("<strong>", "</strong>") },
            { "*", ("<em>", "</em>") },
            { "~~", ("<del>", "</del>") }
        };
    }

    protected override string ApplyPostProcessing(string \
text)
    {
        foreach (var key in tagsToReplace.Keys)
        {
            var replacementTags = tagsToReplace[key];

            if (CountStringOccurrences(text, key) % 2 == \
0)
                text = ApplyTagReplacement(text, key, rep\
lacementTags.Item1, replacementTags.Item2);
        }

        return text;
    }
```

```
36      private int CountStringOccurrences(string text, strin\
37  g pattern)
38      {
39          int count = 0;
40          int currentIndex = 0;
41          while ((currentIndex = text.IndexOf(pattern, curr\
42  entIndex)) != -1)
43          {
44              currentIndex += pattern.Length;
45              count++;
46          }
47          return count;
48      }
49
50      private string ApplyTagReplacement(string text, strin\
51  g inputTag, string outputOpeningTag, string outputClosing\
52  Tag)
53      {
54          int count = 0;
55          int currentIndex = 0;
56
57          while ((currentIndex = text.IndexOf(inputTag, cur\
58  rentIndex)) != -1)
59          {
60              count++;
61
62              if (count % 2 != 0)
63              {
64                  var prepend = outputOpeningTag;
65                  text = text.Insert(currentIndex, prepend);
66                  currentIndex += prepend.Length + inputTag\
67  .Length;
68              }
69              else
70              {
```

```
71                    var append = outputClosingTag;
72                    text = text.Insert(currentIndex, append);
73                    currentIndex += append.Length + inputTag.\
74 Length;
75                }
76            }
77
78            return text.Replace(inputTag, string.Empty);
79        }
80 }
```

Now, we can test both implementations. To do so, we will replace the content of the Program.cs file with the following:

```
1  using Template_Method_Demo;
2
3  var inputText = @"This is the *first* paragraph.
4  This is the **second** paragraph.
5  This is the ~~third~~ paragraph.";
6
7  Console.WriteLine("Text after using basic converter:");
8  var basicTextConverter = new BasicTextToHtmlConverter();
9  Console.WriteLine(basicTextConverter.ConvertText(inputTex\
10 t));
11
12 Console.WriteLine("Text after using MD converter:");
13 var mdToHtmlConverter = new MdToHtmlConverter();
14 Console.WriteLine(mdToHtmlConverter.ConvertText(inputText\
15 ));
16
17 Console.ReadKey();
```

And, as expected, BasicTextToHtmlConverter has left all the MD markers intact. The MdToHtmlConverter, on the other hand, has correctly identified them all and replaced each with a corresponding HTML tag.

```
Text after using basic converter:
<p>This is the *first* paragraph.</p>
<p>This is the **second** paragraph.</p>
<p>This is the ~~third~~ paragraph.</p>
<br/>

Text after using MD converter:
<p>This is the <em>first</em> paragraph.</p>
<p>This is the <strong>second</strong> paragraph.</p>
<p>This is the <del>third</del> paragraph.</p>
<br/>
```

Figure 44.2 - Different outcomes with different implementations of Template Method

And this concludes the overview of the Template Method design pattern. Let's now summarize its benefits.

Benefits of using Template Method

The main benefits of using Template Method are as follows:

- It's easy to define a structure for related algorithms.
- Open-closed principle is well maintained, as the original class doesn't have to change.
- You can reuse code in related algorithms without having to write similar steps.

And now we will have a look at the things to watch out for while using Template Method.

Caveats of using Template Method

One thing you need to be mindful of while using Template Method is making sure that you don't violate the Liskov substitution principle, as it's an easy principle to accidentally violate while using this design pattern.

Also, you need to make sure that the process inside the Template Method doesn't have too many steps. Otherwise you will be violating the single responsibility principle and perhaps even making your code more difficult to maintain overall.

45. Visitor

Visitor is a design pattern that allows you to modify the behavior of existing objects when you cannot modify these objects directly. Essentially, you allow these objects to be "visited" by an external object. This object would call one of the public methods on the original object. But either before or after the call, it will perform some additional actions.

Visitor design pattern can be summarized as follows:

- The original object is known as **Component**.
- **Visitor** object has a method that would call a specific method on a specific implementation of **Component** while performing some additional actions.
- **Component** implementation has been extended to accept a **Visitor** object.
- When a **Visitor** object is accepted by a **Component** object, the specific method on **Visitor** object gets triggered.

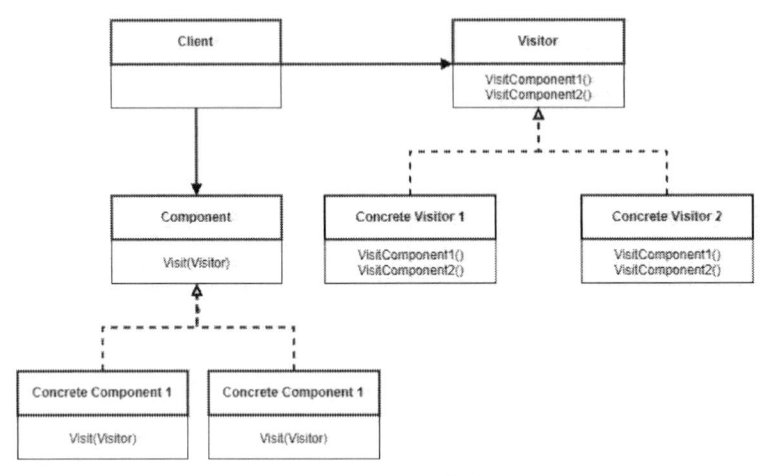

Figure 45.1 - Visitor UML diagram

We will now go through an example implementation of Visitor. The complete solution can be found via the link below:

https://github.com/fiodarsazanavets/design-patterns-in-csharp/tree/main/Behavioral_Patterns/Visitor

Prerequisites

In order to be able to implement the code samples below, you need the following installed on your machine:

- .NET 6 SDK (or newer)
- A suitable IDE or a code editor (Visual Studio, Visual Studio Code, JetBrains Rider)

Visitor implementation example

Imagine that we had a library that is capable of converting between some basic HTML and plain text. However, we then realize that it doesn't deal with all HTML element types. And then we also realize that we don't want to just deal with plain text. We want to convert between HTML and Markdown.

But the problem is that we can't change the original functionality, as this will break some components of the system that is already using it. So, we call the Visitor design pattern to our rescue.

We will create a console application project. Then we will add the following interface to it to enable our existing classes to accept a **Visitor**.

```
1  namespace Visitor_Demo;
2
3  internal interface IComponent
4  {
5      string Accept(IVisitor visitor, string text);
6  }
```

To fix the compiler error that complains about the absence of the IVisitor type, we add this type. And it will look as follows:

```
1  namespace Visitor_Demo;
2
3  internal interface IVisitor
4  {
5      string VisitTextToHtmlConverter(TextToHtmlConverter c\
6  omponent, string text);
7      string VisitHtmlToTextConverter(HtmlToTextConverter c\
8  omponent, string text);
9  }
```

In this **Visitor** interface, we have methods that will allow us to visit two concrete **Component** objects. And we will now add both of these objects.

HtmlToTextConverter class will have the following definition:

```
1   namespace Visitor_Demo;
2
3   internal class HtmlToTextConverter : IComponent
4   {
5       public string Accept(IVisitor visitor, string text)
6       {
7           return visitor.VisitHtmlToTextConverter(this, tex\
8   t);
9       }
10
11      public string ProcessParagraphs(string text)
12      {
13          return text
14              .Replace("<p>", "")
15              .Replace("</p>", "\n")
16              .Replace("<br/>", "");
17      }
18  }
```

And `TextToHtmlConverter` will look like this:

```
1   using System.Text;
2   using System.Text.RegularExpressions;
3
4   namespace Visitor_Demo;
5
6   internal class TextToHtmlConverter : IComponent
7   {
8       public string Accept(IVisitor visitor, string text)
9       {
10          return visitor.VisitTextToHtmlConverter(this, tex\
11  t);
12      }
13
14      public string ProcessParagraphs(string text)
```

```
15      {
16          var paragraphs = Regex.Split(text, @"(\r\n?|\n)")
17                              .Where(p => p.Any(char.IsLetter\
18  OrDigit));
19
20          var sb = new StringBuilder();
21
22          foreach (var paragraph in paragraphs)
23          {
24              if (paragraph.Length == 0)
25                  continue;
26
27              sb.AppendLine($"<p>{paragraph}</p>");
28          }
29
30          sb.AppendLine("<br/>");
31          return sb.ToString();
32      }
33  }
```

As you can see, these convertors only know how to deal with p and br HTML elements. But we want them both to be able to deal with strong, em and del elements too. Also, we want the converters to be able to convert between these elements and corresponding MD markers. And to apply this functionality, we will add the following **Visitor** implementation:

```csharp
namespace Visitor_Demo;

internal class MdConverterVisitor : IVisitor
{
    public string VisitTextToHtmlConverter(TextToHtmlConv\
erter component, string text)
    {
        text = component.ProcessParagraphs(text);

        var tagsToReplace = new Dictionary<string, (strin\
g, string)>
        {
            { "**", ("<strong>", "</strong>") },
            { "*", ("<em>", "</em>") },
            { "~~", ("<del>", "</del>") }
        };

        foreach (var key in tagsToReplace.Keys)
        {
            var replacementTags = tagsToReplace[key];

            if (CountStringOccurrences(text, key) % 2 == \
0)
                text = ApplyTagReplacement(text, key, rep\
lacementTags.Item1, replacementTags.Item2);
        }

        return text;
    }

    public string VisitHtmlToTextConverter(HtmlToTextConv\
erter component, string text)
    {
        return component.ProcessParagraphs(text)
            .Replace("<strong>", "**")
```

```
36                .Replace("</strong>", "**")
37                .Replace("<em>", "*")
38                .Replace("</em>", "*")
39                .Replace("<del>", "~~")
40                .Replace("</del>", "~~");
41       }
42
43       private int CountStringOccurrences(string text, strin\
44   g pattern)
45       {
46           int count = 0;
47           int currentIndex = 0;
48           while ((currentIndex = text.IndexOf(pattern, curr\
49   entIndex)) != -1)
50           {
51               currentIndex += pattern.Length;
52               count++;
53           }
54           return count;
55       }
56
57       private string ApplyTagReplacement(string text, strin\
58   g inputTag, string outputOpeningTag, string outputClosing\
59   Tag)
60       {
61           int count = 0;
62           int currentIndex = 0;
63
64           while ((currentIndex = text.IndexOf(inputTag, cur\
65   rentIndex)) != -1)
66           {
67               count++;
68
69               if (count % 2 != 0)
70               {
```

```
71                    var prepend = outputOpeningTag;
72                    text = text.Insert(currentIndex, prepend);
73                    currentIndex += prepend.Length + inputTag\
74 .Length;
75                }
76                else
77                {
78                    var append = outputClosingTag;
79                    text = text.Insert(currentIndex, append);
80                    currentIndex += append.Length + inputTag.\
81 Length;
82                }
83            }
84
85            return text.Replace(inputTag, string.Empty);
86        }
87 }
```

And that's it. We have added some new functionality to our existing **Component** objects. And the only modification that we have applied to our **Component** objects was the added ability to accept a **Visitor** object. All remaining functionality remained intact.

Now, we will replace the content of our Program.cs class to test our **Visitor** logic.

```
1  using Visitor_Demo;
2
3  var mdText = @"This is **first** paragraph.
4  This is *second* paragraph.
5  This is ~~third~~ paragraph.";
6
7  var htmlText = @"<p>This is <strong>first</strong> paragr\
8  aph.</p>
9  <p>This is <em>second</em> paragraph.</p>
10 <p>This is <del>third</del> paragraph.</p>
```

```
11      <br/>";
12
13      var visitor = new MdConverterVisitor();
14      var textToHtmlConverter = new TextToHtmlConverter();
15      var htmlToTextConverter = new HtmlToTextConverter();
16
17      Console.WriteLine("MD text converted to HTML:");
18      Console.WriteLine(textToHtmlConverter.Accept(visitor, mdT\
19      ext));
20      Console.WriteLine("");
21      Console.WriteLine("HTML text converted to MD:");
22      Console.WriteLine(htmlToTextConverter.Accept(visitor, htm\
23      lText));
24
25      Console.ReadKey();
```

And, as we can see from the following screenshot, we were successfully able to add some new behavior.

```
MD text converted to HTML:
<p>This is <strong>first</strong> paragraph.</p>
<p>This is <em>second</em> paragraph.</p>
<p>This is <del>third</del> paragraph.</p>
<br/>


HTML text converted to MD:
This is **first** paragraph.

This is *second* paragraph.

This is ~~third~~ paragraph.
```

Figure 45.2 - The outcome of using different Visitors

The overview of the Visitor design pattern is now complete. Let's summarize the value it gives us.

Benefits of using Visitor

Visitor design pattern has the following key benefits:

- A new functionality can be added to existing objects without modifying their existing logic.
- Open-closed principle is well maintained, as the existing objects remain close to modification.

And now let's get familiar with the things that you need to watch out for while using Visitor.

Caveats of using Visitor

So, the main caveat of using the Visitor design pattern is that **Visitor** object doesn't have access to private and protected members of the **Component**. And this makes it unsuitable for certain scenarios where some new functionality needs to be added to an existing object.

Another caveat of using Visitor is that there are times where the **Component** object would be modified. As a developer, you need to watch out for, so you can either update your corresponding **Visitor** or retire it altogether.

Finally, because a **Visitor** object may contain many methods, each corresponding to a specific **Component** implementation, you need to watch out for having too many of such methods on a single **Visitor**. Otherwise, you may end up with a God object.

Epilogue

In this book, you have learned most of the key foundational design patterns. I call them foundational, because these are the classic design patterns that inspired all the other design patterns that you may encounter.

And there was a great value in learning these design patterns. Maybe some of them are almost obsolete. For example, real-life situations where using the classic version of the Singleton design pattern are extremely rare. But the principles behind each of these design patterns still live on.

You may no longer be able to find an appropriate scenario to use the Bridge design pattern in its classic form. But still, this pattern made other, more modern design patterns possible. For example, both Model-View-Controller and Model-View-ViewModel design patterns are based on Bridge. Likewise, Bridge has inspired the modern architecture of distributed applications, where the UI and the back-end API are represented by different applications.

And that's a good example of why I call these design patterns "foundational". Knowing them makes it easy to learn any other design patterns. And it makes it easy to understand many of the modern-day architectural best practices.

So, don't be put off by the fact that you haven't seen things like Model-View-Presenter or Repository in this book. There are many design patterns out there and it's just impossible to cover them all in a single book. But now, since you know the most fundamental ones of them all, you will have absolutely no problem learning any other design patterns that have been invented more recently.

There is only one classic design pattern that we haven't included in this book. And it's called Iterator. But there was a good reason not to include it. First of all, in my entire career at both writing commercial software and looking at open source code, I haven't seen a single example where this design pattern was being used. Not one. Secondly, this design pattern is fairly complex and adds very little value compared to other patterns. Therefore the decision was made to leave it out.

A quick reminder that, if you want to get in touch with me regarding the content of the book, you can contact me via either Twitter or LinkedIn. Perhaps, there is additional content that you want to have included in the next edition of the book. Or maybe you found some errors in the current edition. Any feedback is welcome. And this is how you can get in touch:

Twitter: https://twitter.com/FSazanavets

LinkedIn: https://www.linkedin.com/in/fiodar-sazanavets/

Also, if you found this book useful, please write a review about it on the site you bought it from. This will help me as the author and will help the algorithms to show this book to more people who might need help with learning design patterns.

And, of course, if you liked this book, spread the word. Let your friends know about it. This way, you will help more people to become better software developers.

All the best and good luck!

Printed in Poland
by Amazon Fulfillment
Poland Sp. z o.o., Wrocław
01 August 2023